D1553495

Pitt Press Series

P. OVIDII NASONIS

FASTORUM

LIBER VI

CAMBRIDGE UNIVERSITY PRESS

C. F. CLAY, Manager

LONDON : FETTER LANE, E.C. 4

NEW YORK : THE MACMILLAN CO.
BOMBAY
CALCUTTA } MACMILLAN AND CO., Ltd.
MADRAS
TORONTO : THE MACMILLAN CO. OF
CANADA, Ltd.
TOKYO: MARUZEN-KABUSHIKI-KAISHA

P. OVIDII NASONIS

FASTORUM

LIBER VI

EDITED BY

A. SIDGWICK, M.A.

CAMBRIDGE

AT THE UNIVERSITY PRESS

1921

First Edition 1877
Reprinted 1878 (*twice*), 1880, 1883, 1886, 1888, 1890, 1894,
1900, 1903, 1921

PREFATORY NOTE.

THIS Edition, being prepared for the use of those Students
who are not far advanced in Latin, does not aim at doing more
than supplying in a small compass such help to the thorough
knowledge of this book as it is probable would be most useful
to them. It is not intended to supply the place of a dictionary :
for all students possess one, and derive much benefit from its
careful use, both in becoming acquainted with the *history of
meanings* of words, and also in the exercise of that judgment
which is required to select the right meaning. On the other
hand historical and mythical allusions are explained in the
notes, as many students might find it difficult to make them out
otherwise. Great care also has been taken to notice all the
grammatical usages which might offer any difficulty, and to
classify them clearly, and to enable the learner, by means of an
Index (and Scheme of the uses of the Subjunctive), to compare
and distinguish the various usages. The reader's attention has
also been drawn here and there to the special peculiarities of
style.

The book being full of allusions to temples, buildings, hills,
roads, &c., in Rome, it has been thought best to prepare a small
sketch-map, containing all the places or buildings alluded to in
the book. The scale of the Map has rendered it desirable to omit
all details, except those which are mentioned in the Text. This
will make the Map much clearer, and easier to use. The leading features have obviously been retained.

The Text adopted has been mainly that of Rudolph Merkel,
Leipzig, 1876. In one or two places I have however adopted

the corrections of other editors or scholars, such as Madvig, Bentley, and Peter.

The book which has been most useful to me in the preparation of the notes has been Ovid's *Fasti für die Schule erklärt*, von Hermann Peter, Leipzig, 1874 : an admirable commentary which with its Critical Appendix supplies nearly every need of the reader of Ovid.

I have also consulted on many points Merkel's Prolegomena to Ovid's *Fasti* (Berlin, 1841), a learned and exhaustive but needlessly tedious book.

For the topography of Rome, and for help in constructing the Map, I have been indebted to the magnificent work on 'Rome and the Campagna,' by the Rev. Robert Burn, of Trinity College, Cambridge. The constant use I have made of it has only brought out more clearly to me the extreme accuracy and thoroughness with which it is written.

I have given two Indices : an Index of grammar and general matters ; and an Index of names. The latter has been thought desirable, owing to the large number of allusions in the book.

[N. B. In one or two places expurgations have been necessary, and I have omitted the unfit passages, altering occasionally a word or two, to keep the connexion clear. In all cases the original numbers have been retained, as otherwise there might be a difficulty about references.]

INTRODUCTION.

THE little that needs to be said by way of introduction will be most useful if divided into heads.

These heads are as follows :

§ 1. Outline of the life of Ovid.
§ 2. Ovid's works : date of the Fasti.
§ 3. The subject of the Fasti.
§ 4. The Reformation of the Calendar.
§ 5. The Classification of the days.
§ 6. The Astronomy of Ovid.
§ 7. A List of Gods.

The scheme of the subjunctive will be found at the end of the notes, before the two Indices.

§ 1. *Outline of the life of Ovid.*

Publius Ovidius Naso (the surname means 'the big-nosed', being originally a nickname, no doubt, like many of the Roman cognomina, though they were regularly continued in the same family, and often, like Cicero, Brutus, Scipio, carried only the most honourable associations) was born 20 March 43, just one year after Julius Caesar's murder. His father had a farm at Sulmo, in the country of the Peligni (about the centre of the hills E. of Rome) and the boy was brought up as a lawyer. It is said, as might be expected from the turn of his genius, that he was a good

..mer, but a bad pleader. He studied finally, like so many
.. the educated Romans of the time, at Athens, where he
became an accomplished Greek scholar; and afterwards travelled
in Asia and Sicily. He tells us himself that his bent was all for
poetry; and his chief friends were the poets of the time. He
was acquainted with Propertius, Gallus, Ponticus, Bassus, Macer,
and Horace. Vergil 'he only just saw' (Trist. IV. 10. 51): for
Vergil spent his last years either at Naples or abroad, and died
when Ovid was only 24. He was appointed a judge after his return
to Rome, and ultimately became one of the decemviri or Bench of
Ten who presided over certain trials. He divorced two wives and
appears to have married a third time more happily. He lived in
the best literary society at Rome, and enjoyed for several years
the friendship of Augustus. In A. D. 8 however, he offended the
court and was banished for the rest of his life to Tomi, a Greek
colony on the Euxine, in the Dobrudscha, that dreary region S.
of the Danube-mouths. The ostensible ground for this exile
was said to have been the immoral Love-poem (Ars Amatoria)
which he had published 10 years before. The real ground is
unknown: and in the absence of information has been supposed
to be some profligate intrigue. In his banishment he wrote the
Tristia and Letters from the Pontus, in which he gives the
most piteous account of the dangers and discomforts of his life
in that wretched country, interspersed with servile flattery of
Augustus and plaintive entreaties to his friends to get him
recalled. They, however, either did not try, or failed; and he
died in exile A. D. 18.

§ 2. *Ovid's works: Date of the Fasti.*

Ovid began his poetic career with poems of love, in the
Elegiac metre, in which the elder poets Tibullus and Propertius
were already famous. But his chief model is said to have been
a Greek Parthenius, who was taken prisoner as a child in the
war with Mithridates (ended 63 B.C.) and who was set free at
Rome on account of his talents. Ovid's first works were the

Amores, the *Heroides* (or 'Love-Letters of the Heroines,' Medea, Sappho, &c.) and the 'Art of Love.' Then came the *Remedia Amoris* and *Nux*. Then the *Metamorphoses*, a long work of 15 books in hexameters: it consists of Legends of Transformations, without any special connection. It may have been effective to recite to a Roman audience, in parts : but it is not to be called an epic, though apparently aspiring to be one. Then the XII books of *Fasti*, or 'Versified calendar,' a book for each month : of which only six, however, remain. In exile, as we have said, he wrote the *Tristia*, or 'Elegies of Lament' and 'Letters from Pontus.' There are besides one or two minor works extant, and some which are lost : of the latter a tragedy on 'Medea' is the most famous.

As to the date of the Fasti, it is probable that the six books we have were all written before he left Rome : for even if he could have had the necessary materials at Tomi, he could scarcely have had the desire or the energy to continue a work intended to glorify the Rome which he had lost and the Emperor whom he had grievously offended. One or two passages, it is true, must have been written at Tomi, as IV. 82 (me miserum ! Scythico quam procul illa solo est ! &c.): but both the general tone, the absence of any mention of the Fasti in the Epistles from Tomi, the language used about Caesar, and many minor indications (cf. VI. 666), shew that the work was practically written before, and no doubt dedicated to Augustus, to whom allusions are frequent.

However in A.D. 14 Augustus died. Ovid had no hope from Tiberius, his successor, of being suffered to return from banishment.

But in 16 the jealousy of Tiberius recalled the victorious Germanicus (his adopted son) from Germany, and sent him to the East. Germanicus was known to be a cultivated man : and it was then probably that Ovid recast his first book into its present shape, and prefaced it with a laudatory address to Germanicus. The passage in IV. 80, alluded to above, was then probably written. But most of the allusions to Augustus are left unaltered.

§ 3.   *On the subject of the Fasti.*

This is not the place to treat of the extraordinary burst of literature which appeared in the reign of Augustus, nor to discuss the question how far the enthusiasm for the court and the new epoch, which the poets of the time express, was servile and artificial, or how far it was a genuine belief that 'a good time was come.' Probably both the true and the false were there, and different men felt to a different degree what it was the fashion for all to enlarge upon. After the desolating civil wars of the last century, it may well be that the imagination of all Rome was really stirred by the spectacle of a universal peace, and the hope that a new period of national greatness and prosperity had begun.

There is no doubt that it was the aim of the sagacious Emperor to revive on all sides as much as possible the national sentiment, which had been much impaired by the breakdown of the senatorial government, latterly so corrupt and incapable, and by the class bitterness which the civil strife and frequent proscriptions had evoked and exasperated. And to nothing did he pay more attention than to a revival of the national religion. He rebuilt and restored the temples : revived the old worships : encouraged the celebration of the various games, always originally in honour of some god : devoted large treasure to the various shrines ; increased the number and dignity of the priests ; and put himself at the head of the movement by permanently accepting the office of Pontifex Maximus.

The official register of the holy-days and festivals was the calendar, which, hitherto under the exclusive control of the priests, now became part of the emperor's care. Nothing could better help the policy of Augustus than the work of popularising the calendar and adorning it with poetic treatment. This was the task which Ovid undertook in the *Fasti.* The calendar moreover was the especial glory of the Caesarian house. It was one of the greatest works of Julius Caesar, (as is explained fully in the next section), to reform the errors and confusion into which the priestly management had brought it. To the completion and establishment of this reform Augustus himself had contributed. The poet's subject was therefore in two ways appropriate to the time. It was also eminently suited to his genius. He was incapable of a sustained poetical effort, or a grand conception, like Vergil's Aeneid: his 'Metamorphoses' are clear proof of this. His strength lay in neatness of expression, in light and graceful writing, in simple clear and rapid narrative. The desultory nature of his subject, requiring ingenuity to avoid tedious repetition, and giving scope to his story-telling faculty, was therefore not merely no obstacle, it was an advantage to him. And this is why, in spite of the seemingly unpromising subject, no work of his has been more read, or more famous.

The Fasti is accordingly a 'versified calendar.' Each Book treats of one month; and our book being the sixth contains the account of June. Ovid as far as possible explains the calendar-signs attached to each day: gives a narrative of the events commemorated, the founding of temples, the thanksgiving for victories, the stories of the gods or heroes worshipped, and the ceremonies in use. He is especially fond of tracing back the origin of names and usages: such explanations giving scope to his ingenuity and inventiveness, for of scientific antiquarian research he of course has no idea. He also gives astronomical information; and relates the rising and setting of different constellations on different days. Presumably this is done with the view of being useful, as such a calendar would be, to farmers and sailors. It may however have been simply that a calendar would not have been complete without it[1]; and that it was a kind of subject well adapted to his purpose, as it enabled him to bring in the endless legends, chiefly of Greek origin, connected with the stars. Anyhow, the astronomy was not a scientific success; as will be explained below, (§ 6).

[1] Julius Caesar's Calendar apparently contained some astronomical notices.

§ 4.   *The Reformation of the Calendar.*

One of the greatest services rendered by Julius Caesar to the Empire and the world was the reformation of the Calendar. Before his time the year consisted of 355 days, and every two years an intercalary month was inserted (between the 23rd and the 24th of February) of 22 or 23 days. This process made the year too long, and as the error of course mounted up it became observable that the nominal seasons no longer coincided with the actual ones. The regulation of the calendar was in the hands of the pontifices, and they accordingly exercised their right of altering the intercalation to suit the solar year. But during the later years of the republic their administration, like every other, became incapable and corrupt ; and they used to lengthen or shorten the calendar to serve or spite some magistrate or taxfarmer who chanced to have won their favour or hate. Add to this the complete disorganization of everything during the civil wars ; and by the time of Julius Caesar we find the nominal year was more than 2 months in advance of the solar seasons. Thus Caesar in his history of the civil war after describing (III. 6) how the fleet set sail on the 31st of December says three chapters further on (III. 9) 'the winter was now approaching'! We are not surprised to be told by Suetonius (Caes. 40) that 'the harvest festivals did not coincide with the summer nor the vintage with the autumn.'

Caesar having obtained supreme power set himself, among other reforms, to put this confusion straight. He had mastered some knowledge of astronomy, sufficient for his purpose, and obtained the aid of the philosopher Sosigenes. In B.C. 46, which had already received the intercalation of 23 days in February, he added 67 days in two intercalary months inserted between November and December. Cicero writing to Ligarius (Fam. VI. 14) refers to this arrangement, when he says he visited Caesar 'a. d. v. Kalendas intercalares priores,' i.e. Nov. 26, or 'five days (we should say *four*) before the first of the first intercalary month.' Thus the year 46 contained 445 days, and is fitly called by Macrobius 'the last year of confusion.' For the future Caesar dispensed with the intercalary month, distributing ten days among the seven months which had only had 29, viz. Jan. Apr. June, Aug. Sept. Nov. giving two to Jan. Aug. and Dec., and the rest one. This made the year 365 days long, about a quarter of a day too short : and this latter error he remedied by the intercalation of one day after Feb. 23 every fourth year. It was placed there, and not at the end, because the last five days were regarded in some way as extra to the year ; the 23 Feb. being the Terminalia or Last Day, as the 1st March had always been New year's day[1]. This is our present arrangement, except that we count the 29th as the intercalary day.

It should be mentioned that there was still an error in the Julian calculation, which estimated the solar year at $365\frac{1}{4}$ days ; for this is really in excess of the true year by more than 11 minutes. Caesar either was unaware of this, or he thought it might be disregarded. But as time went on, the error accumulated, and in 1582 it had amounted to 13 days. Pope Gregory XIII again reformed the calendar, striking out ten of the thirteen days, and arranging to avoid the error for the future by leaving out three leap-years in every four centuries. Thus 1700, 1800, and 1900 are not leap-years, but 2000 is ; and so on. This arrangement is known as the New Style, and was adopted in England in 1752.

§ 5. *The Classification of the Days.*

Dies fasti were properly 'Speaking-days' or days on which the praetor could 'speak,' (i.e. could use the three legal words 'do, dico, addico,' 'I give, pronounce, award') and so, days on which legal business could be carried on.

---

[1] In the leap-year, accordingly, the old days' names were kept, the 25th being (as the 24th was usually) a. d. VI. Kal. Mart., and the 24th in this year was a. d. VI. Kal. Mart. *posterior*, the other being *prior*. Thus there were two *sexti* or 6th days, and hence the term Bissextile.

The calendar was called 'Fasti' because these days were the most important. The subdivision of days was as follows :

I. *Dies fasti* in general sense, 'business days,' consisting of:

    1. *dies fasti* in the special sense, as above : marked F in the Calendar.

    2. *dies comitiales*, or days on which Senate or People could be assembled. If there were no comitia, then they became *fasti* proper. The *nundinae* or market days, which fell every eighth (they said *ninth*) day were always *Comitiales*: but these could not be marked in the calendar as they naturally were different each year : the other *Comitiales* were marked C.

II. *Dies nefasti*, days when no business could be done :

    1. days marked NP, which were sacred to the gods.

    2. days marked N, which were unlucky or 'black' (*atri*). Such were the days after Calends, Nones and Ides.

III. Mixed days, as :—

    1. days marked EN, *intercisi* (anciently endo = in) or 'interrupted' days.

    2. days marked Q. R. C. F. or '*quando rex comitiavit fas*' 'after the rex sacrificulus has been to the forum, business may be done.'

    3. the 15 June (see notes on 227) marked Q. ST. D. F or '*quando stercus delatum, fas*,' ' when the dirt is carried away, business may be done.'

See Ovid I. 45—60.
The above list is mainly from H. Peter's edition.

§ 6. *On the Astronomy of Ovid.*

We have seen that Julius Caesar's Calendar contained some notices of the rising and setting of stars and constellations. Such notices had been from the earliest times recorded in Greece, where the climate permitted shepherds to be out with their flocks all night, and where one of the earliest forms of literature was the agricultural poem of Hesiod. After a while rural almanacks began to be formed, and the phenomena were observed with as much care as possible. At Rome the process of intercalating the alternate years must have made much more difficult the work of attaching special stars to special days, as the irregularity of the civil calendar would render such a work either very vague (allowing a margin of several days) very complex (different for different years) or altogether confused. We are not therefore surprised to find that the Julian Calendar (by which intercalation was confined to one day every four years) was made a new departure for the record of these astronomical observations. With care, the record might have been very fairly accurate, and really useful. Unfortunately however Ovid's purpose was far more literary than scientific : and the poet was clearly not qualified, as Julius Caesar had taken pains to qualify himself, for the astronomical part of his work. Whether, as some have argued[1], he derived his notices of the stars chiefly from a contemporary student, Clodius Tuscus, or whether he made indiscriminate use of various and conflicting materials, it is not worth while to decide, even if it were possible. The plain fact is that his statements are oftener wrong than right : and the total result to anyone who tried to make practical use of his tables must have been confusion worse confounded.

It will not be difficult to make this clear, by shewing what main sources of error there were, in speaking of the stars, to a poet who was no astronomer.

1. It is necessary to distinguish the *morning* rising or setting from the *evening* rising or setting.

[1] Merkel, Prolegomena, LXV. sqq.

In popular language when we speak of a star rising, we mean a phenomenon which recurs every 24 hours. If a star rises one night, it also rises the next, and so on. The phenomenon here spoken of is not a daily, but a yearly one. When it is stated that on such a day the Pleiades *rise in the morning*, the meaning is that on that day the Pleiades rise with the sun, that is, at the moment of sunrise. This can only happen once in the year. So the day when a star *sets in the morning* is the day when it sets at sunrise; and similarly the *evening rising* and *setting* mean the rising and setting at sunset. It is clearly of the first importance to distinguish whether it is at sunrise or sunset. There is no doubt that in the Fasti these are occasionally confused.

2. It is necessary to distinguish the *true* rising from the *apparent* or *heliacal* rising.

As long as the sun is up, the stars cannot be seen: and when we speak of a star rising *at sunrise or sunset* we mean in the twilight, *a little before sunrise*, or a *little after sunset*. In the rustic almanacks this alone would be entered, as this alone would be useful. But it was not difficult for even the earliest astronomers to calculate the *true* rising, or the day when the star rose exactly at sunrise or sunset. The Greek astronomer Geminus (c. 80 B.C.) knows all about it, and in many of the more elaborate calendars this would be the rising intended.

This distinction Ovid never mentions, and he plainly has no idea of it, quoting his authorities without suspicion that the two differ from each other, and that he ought to know which he is talking of.

3. The calculations and observations made elsewhere (in Greece, Egypt, &c.) would have to be corrected, if they were to be used at Rome, for differences of latitude.

Of this Ovid knows nothing.

4. Owing to a slight movement of the earth's axis (Precession of the Equinoxes), the observations true for a certain time, say 500 B.C. would be no longer true in Ovid's day. Thus the divisions of the Zodiac, or the sun's apparent path among

the stars, originally of course corresponded to the constellations whence the names of the signs were taken. In Ovid's day they no longer did so. The error would affect other constellations also.

Of this too he knows nothing.

5. Even the names of the constellations are occasionally confused. Thus (IV. 904) he confuses Canis and Canicula.

6. To all these sources of error it is highly probable that Ovid adds another, which might be the greatest of all : namely, that he at times is using older calculations without making the necessary changes for the *reformed calendar.*

The references to astronomy in this book will bear out the conclusions thus arrived at. The following statements are made :

(1)	Line 196.	June 1.	The eagle rises (he does not say whether morning or evening).
(2)	„ 197.	June 2.	Hyades rise in the morning.
(3)	„ 235.	June 7.	Arctophylax sets in the morning.
(4)	„ 469.	June 10.	Dolphin rises in the evening.
(5)	„ 711.	June 15.	Hyades rise in the morning.
(6)	„ 719.	June 16.	Orion's arm rises in the evening.
(7)	„ 720.	June 17.	Dolphin rises in the evening.
(8)	„ 735.	June 20.	Ophiuchus rises in the evening.
(9)	„ 785.	June 26.	Orion's belt rises (he means probably) in the morning.

We observe at once that two of these, the Hyades and the Dolphin, are mentioned as rising *twice*, at the same time on two different days, which is clearly impossible.

Let us take them in order :

(1) The rising referred to is the true evening one, and the day is *right.*

(2) and (5). The apparent morning rising of the Hyades was the 9th June : so (2) is seven days too soon, (5) is six days too late. *Both wrong.*

(3) The apparent morning setting of Arcturus (the brightest star in Arctophylax) is 10 June: as the whole constellation takes some time to set, this is fairly *right.*

(4) and (7). The true evening rising is 10 June: so (4) is *right*, (7) a week *wrong*.

(6) The actual *morning* rising of Orion's arm was 16 June: but Ovid says it was the *evening* rising, and *is wrong*.

(8) The *apparent evening rising* of Ophiuchus was 19 April: but Ovid is probably confusing it with the *true morning setting*, which was on 21 June. In either case, *wrong*.

(9) The true morning rising of the Belt was 21 June: so Ovid is five days *wrong*.

We observe therefore here :

a.   In no case does he say whether it **is** the true or the apparent time he is speaking of : though it is sometimes one, sometimes the other.

b.   In two cases he gives a double date, which is absurd.

c.   In two cases he confuses the morning with the evening, (6) and (8).

d.   In one case (8) he confuses the setting with the rising.

e.   In four cases, even where he means the right phenomenon, the date is wrong.

[The information given above is derived partly from a masterly article on Ancient Astronomy, by the late Professor W. Ramsay, of Glasgow, in Dr Smith's Antiquities' Dictionary : and partly from Peter's Critical Appendix. Both are founded mainly on an exhaustive treatise, by Ideler, on the Astronomy of Ovid's Fasti.]

§ 7.   *List of Gods.*

It may be useful to some beginners just to **put** down a list of the chief Roman gods, with the Greek names with which they were identified, or from which they were derived.

ROMAN.	GREEK.
Saturnus, father of Iuppiter,	Kronos.
Iuppiter, king of gods,	Zeus.
Iuno, his sister and wife,	Here.
Neptunus, god of the sea,	Poseidon.

ROMAN.	GREEK.
Pluto or *Dis*, god of the lower world,	Hades or Plouton.
Volcanus, god of fire,	Hephaistos.
Mars, god of war,	Ares.
Mercurius, messenger of the gods,	Hermes.
Apollo or *Phoebus*, god of the lyre, the bow, and the sunlight,	the same, Apollon or Phoibos.
Bacchus, god of wine,	Dionusos or Bacchos.
Aesculapius, god of healing,	Asklepios.
Minerva, goddess of learning,	Athene or Pallas.
Diana, goddess of chastity and hunting,	Artemis.
Venus, goddess of love,	Aphrodite.
Ceres, goddess of corn,	Demeter.
Vesta, goddess of the hearth,	Hestia.
Aurora, the dawn,	Eos.
Sol, the sun,	Helios.
Latona, mother of Apollo and Diana,	Leto.
Hercules, the strong,	Herakles.

For the identification of Greek and Roman deities, see note on 287, and Index.

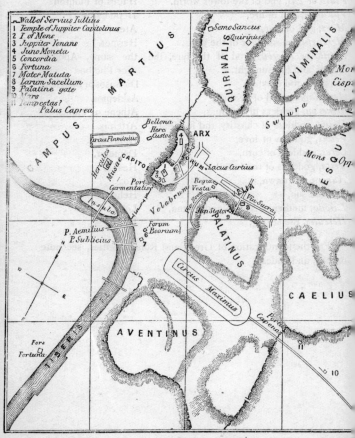

PLAN OF ROME, TO ILLUSTRATE OVID'S FASTI, BOOK

P. OVIDII NASONIS

FASTORUM

LIBER VI.

EXPLANATIONS OF THE NAME JUNE.

1. *From Iuno.   The goddess appears to the poet*

Hic quoque mensis habet dubias in nomine causas:
    Quae placeant, positis omnibus ipse leges.
Facta canam. sed erunt, qui me finxisse loquantur,
    Nullaque mortali numina visa putent.
Est deus in nobis! agitante calescimus illo: 5
    Impetus hic sacrae semina mentis habet.
Fas mihi praecipue voltus vidisse deorum,
    Vel quia sum vates, vel quia sacra cano.
Est nemus arboribus densum, secretus ab omn'
    Voce locus, si non obstreperetur aquis.   10
Hic ego quaerebam, coepti quae mensis origo
    Esset, et in cura nominis huius eram.
Ecce deas vidi: non quas praeceptor arandi
    Viderat, Ascraeas cum sequeretur oves:
Nec quas Priamides in aquosae vallibus Idae   15
    Contulit. ex illis sed tamen una fuit.
Ex illis fuit una, sui germana mariti:
    Haec erat, agnovi, quae stat in arce Iovis.
Horrueram, tacitoque animum pallore fatebar.
    Tum dea, quos fecit, sustulit ipsa metus.   20

2—2

She claims that the month's name is derived from her: she has
deserved it by her rank and favours to Rome.

Namque ait 'O vates, Romani conditor anni,
  'Ause per exiguos magna referre modos,
'Ius tibi fecisti numen caeleste videndi,
  'Cum placuit numeris condere festa tuis.
'Ne tamen ignores volgique errore traharis,   25
  'Iunius a nostro nomine nomen habet.
'Est aliquid nupsisse Iovi, Iovis esse sororem.
  'Fratre magis, dubito, glorier, anne viro.
'Si genus aspicitur, Saturnum prima parentem
  'Feci: Saturni sors ego prima fui.   30
'A patre dicta meo quondam Saturnia Roma est:
  'Haec illi a caelo proxima terra fuit.
'Si torus in pretio est, dicor matrona Tonantis,
  'Iunctaque Tarpeio sunt mea templa Iovi.
'An potuit Maio pelex dare nomina mensi,   35
  'Hic honor in nobis invidiosus erit?
'Cur igitur regina vocor princepsque dearum?
  'Aurea cur dextrae sceptra dedere meae?
'An facient mensem luces, Lucinaque ab illis
  'Dicar, et a nullo nomina mense traham?   40
'Tum me paeniteat posuisse fideliter iras
  'In genus Electrae Dardaniamque domum.
'Causa duplex irae. rapto Ganymede dolebam:
  'Forma quoque Idaeo iudice victa mea est.
'Paeniteat, quod non foveo Carthaginis arces,   45
  'Cum mea sint illo currus et arma loco.
'Paeniteat Sparten Argosque measque Mycenas
  'Et veterem Latio supposuisse Samon.
'Adde senem Tatium, Iunonicolasque Faliscos,
  'Quos ego Romanis succubuisse tuli.   50

'Sed neque paeniteat, nec gens mihi carior ulla est.
  'Hic colar, hic teneam cum Iove templa meo.
'Ipse mihi Mavors "Commendo moenia" dixit
  '"Haec tibi. tu pollens urbe nepotis eris."
'Dicta fides sequitur. centum celebramur in aris :   55
  'Nec levior quovis est mihi mensis honor.
'Nec tamen hunc nobis tantummodo praestat honorem
  'Roma. suburbani dant mihi munus idem.
'Inspice, quos habeat nemoralis Aricia fastos,
  'Et populus Laurens Lanuviumque meum :   60
'Est illic mensis Iunonius. Inspice Tibur
  'Et Praenestinae moenia sacra deae :
'Iunonale leges tempus. Nec Romulus illas
  'Condidit. at nostri Roma nepotis erat.'

2. *From* 'iuvenes.' *Hebe likewise appears and pleads for her-
      self, and the* youth *over whom she presides.*

Finierat Iuno. Respeximus. Herculis uxor   65
  Stabat, et in voltu signa doloris erant.
'Non ego, si toto mater me cedere caelo
  'Iusserit, invita matre morabor' ait.
'Nunc quoque non luctor de nomine temporis huius :
  'Blandior, et partes paene rogantis ago,   70
'Remque mei iuris malim tenuisse precando :
  'Et faveas causae forsitan ipse meae.
'Aurea possedit socio Capitolia templo
  'Mater, et ut debet, cum Iove summa tenet.
'At decus omne mihi contingit origine mensis.   75
  'Unicus est, de quo sollicitamur, honor.
'Quid grave, si titulum mensis, Romane, dedisti
  'Herculis uxori, posteritasque memor?
'Haec quoque terra aliquid debet mihi nomine magni
  'Coniugis. huc captas appulit ille boves.   80

'Hic male defensus flammis et dote paterna
  'Cacus Aventinam sanguine tinxit humum.
'Ad propiora vocor. Populum digessit ab annis
  'Romulus, in partes distribuitque duas.
'Haec dare consilium, pugnare paratior illa est: 85
  'Haec aetas bellum suadet, at illa gerit.
'Sic statuit, mensesque nota secrevit eadem.
  'Iunius est iuvenum. qui fuit ante, senum.'
Dixit. Et in litem studio certaminis issent,
  Atque ira pietas dissimulata foret...   90

3. *From* 'iunctus.' *Concordia appears, and claims the origin
    of the name from the* union *of Sabines and Romans.*

Venit Apollinea longas Concordia lauro
  Nexa comas, placidi numen opusque ducis.
Haec ubi narravit Tatium fortemque Quirinum
  Binaque cum populis regna coisse suis,
Et lare communi soceros generosque receptos,   95
  'His nomen iunctis Iunius' inquit 'habet.'
Dicta triplex causa est. At vos ignoscite, divae:
  Res est arbitrio non dirimenda meo.
Ite pares a me. perierunt iudice formae
  Pergama. plus laedunt, quam iuvet una, duae.   100

THE CALENDAR OF THE MONTH.

1 *June. Feast of Carna. Story of how Ianus loved her, and
    gave her his power.*

Prima dies tibi, Carna, datur. Dea cardinis haec est:
  Numine clausa aperit, claudit aperta suo.
Unde datas habeat vires, obscurior aevo
  Fama; sed e nostro carmine certus eris.

Adiacet antiquus Tiberino lucus Helerni: 105
　　Pontifices illuc nunc quoque sacra ferunt.
Inde sata est nymphe—Granen dixere priores—
　　Nequiquam multis saepe petita procis.
Rura sequi iaculisque feras agitare solebat,
　　Nodosasque cava tendere valle plagas. 110
Non habuit pharetram: Phoebi tamen esse sororem
　　Credebant. nec erat, Phoebe, pudenda tibi.
Huic aliquis iuvenum dixisset amantia verba,
　　Reddebat tales protinus illa sonos:
'Haec loca lucis habent nimis, et cum luce pudoris. 115
'Si secreta magis ducis in antra, sequor.
Credulus ante ut iit, frutices haec nacta resistit,
　　Et latet, et nullo est invenienda modo.
Viderat hanc Ianus; visaeque cupidine captus
　　Ad duram verbis mollibus usus erat. 120
Nympha iubet quaeri de more remotius antrum,
　　Utque comes sequitur, destituitque ducem.
Stulta! videt Ianus, quae post sua terga gerantur:
　　Nil agis, et latebras respicit ille tuas.
Occupat, et tandem: 'munus tibi cardinis esto:· 125
　　'Hoc pretium nostri detur amoris,' ait.

With the thorn that he gives her she drives the screech-owls
from the house of Proca.

Sic fatus spinam, qua tristes pellere posset
　　A foribus noxas—haec erat alba—dedit. 130
Sunt avidae volucres, non quae Phineïa mensis
　　Guttura fraudabant, sed genus inde trahunt:
Grande caput, stantes oculi, rostra apta rapinis:
　　Canities pinnis, unguibus hamus inest.
Nocte volant, puerosque petunt nutricis egentes, 135
　　Et vitiant cunis corpora rapta suis.

Carpere dicuntur lactentia viscera rostris,
  Et plenum poto sanguine guttur habent.
Est illis strigibus nomen. sed nominis huius
  Causa, quod horrendum stridere nocte solent.   140
Sive igitur nascuntur aves, seu carmine fiunt,
  Naeniaque in volucres Marsa figurat anus :
In thalamos venere Procae. Proca natus in illis
  Praeda recens avium quinque diebus erat :
Pectoraque exsorbent avidis infantia linguis :   145
  At puer infelix vagit opemque petit.
Territa voce sui nutrix accurrit alumni,
  Et rigido sectas invenit ungue genas.
Quid faceret? color oris erat, qui frondibus olim
  Esse solet seris, quas nova laesit hiems.   150
Pervenit ad Granen, et rem docet. Illa 'Timorem
  'Pone ! tuus sospes' dixit 'alumnus erit.'
Venerat ad cunas. flebant materque paterque :
  'Sistite vos lacrimas, ipsa medebor !' ait.
Protinus arbutea postes ter in ordine tangit   155
  Fronde, ter arbutea limina fronde notat :
Spargit aquis aditus—et aquae medicamen habebant—
  Extaque de porca cruda bimenstre tenet.
Atque ita 'Noctis aves, extis puerilibus' inquit
  'Parcite. pro parvo victima parva cadit.   160
'Cor pro corde, precor, pro fibris sumite fibras.
  'Hanc animam vobis pro meliore damus.'
Sic ubi libavit, prosecta sub aethere ponit,
  Quique assint sacris, respicere illa vetat.
Virgaque Ianalis de spina ponitur alba,   165
  Qua lumen thalamis parva fenestra dabat.
Post illud nec aves cunas violasse feruntur,
  Et rediit, puero, qui fuit ante, color.

Why bacon, beans, and meal are eaten on 1 June.

Pinguia cur illis gustentur larda Kalendis,
      Mixtaque cum calido sit faba farre, rogas?   170
Prisca dea est, aliturque cibis quibus ante solebat,
      Nec petit ascitas luxuriosa dapes.
Piscis adhuc illi populo sine fraude natabat,
      Ostreaque in conchis tuta fuere suis.
Nec Latium norat, quam praebet Ionia dives,   175
      Nec, quae Pygmaeo sanguine gaudet, avem.
Et praeter pinnas nihil in pavone placebat:
      Nec tellus captas miserat arte feras.
Sus erat in pretio. caesa sue festa colebant.
      Terra fabas tantum duraque farra dabat.   180
Quae duo mixta simul sextis quicumque Kalendis
      Ederit, huic laedi viscera posse negant.

The same day is also the festival of the temples of Moneta,
  Mars, and Tempestas: and on that day the Eagle rises.

Arce quoque in summa Iunoni templa Monetae
      Ex voto memorant facta, Camille, tuo.
Ante domus Manli fuerat, qui Gallica quondam   185
      A Capitolino reppulit arma Iove.
Quam bene, di magni! pugna cecidisset in illa,
      Defensor solii, Iuppiter alte, tui!
Vixit, ut occideret damnatus crimine regni.
      Hunc illi titulum longa senecta dabat.   190
Lux eadem Marti festa est, quem prospicit extra
      Appositum Tectae porta Capena viae.
Te quoque, Tempestas, meritam delubra fatemur,
      Cum paene est Corsis obruta classis aquis.
Haec hominum monimenta patent. Si quaeritis astra, 195
      Tunc oritur magni praepes adunca Iovis.

OVIDII FASTORUM

2 June. The Hyades rise.

Postera lux Hyadas, Taurinae cornua frontis,
  Evocat, et multa terra madescit aqua.

3 June. Festival of the Temple of Bellona. Her pillar.

Mane ubi bis fuerit, Phoebusque iteraverit ortus,
  Factaque erit posito rore bis uda seges,　　　　200
Hac sacrata die Tusco Bellona duello
  Dicitur, et Latio prospera semper adest.
Appius est auctor, Pyrrho qui pace negata
  Multum animo vidit, lumine captus erat.
Prospicit a templo summum brevis area Circum　　205
  Est ibi non parvae parva columna notae.
Hinc solet hasta manu, belli praenuntia, mitti,
  In regem et gentes cum placet arma capi.

4 June. Festival of Temple of Hercules Custos.

Altera pars Circi Custode sub Hercule tuta est:
  Quod deus Euboico carmine munus habet.　　　　210
Muneris est tempus, qui Nonas lucifer ante est.
  Si titulum quaeris, Sulla probavit opus.

5 June. Nones: Festival of the Temple of Semo Sancus or Fidius.

Quaerebam, Nonas Sanco, Fidione referrem,
  An tibi, Semo pater. Tum mihi Sancus ait:
'Cuicumque ex istis dederis, ego munus habebo.　　215
  Nomina terna fero. sic voluere Cures.'
Hunc igitur veteres donarunt aede Sabini,
  Inque Quirinali constituere iugo.

Digression. The poet is advised not to celebrate his daughter's marriage before the Ides.

Est mihi—sitque, precor, nostris diuturnior annis—
  Filia, qua felix sospite semper ero.　　　　220

Hanc ego cum vellem genero dare, tempora taedis
　Apta requirebam, quaeque cavenda forent.
Tum mihi post sacras monstratur Iunius Idus
　Utilis et nuptis, utilis esse viris ;
Primaque pars huius thalamis aliena reperta est. 225
　Nam mihi sic coniunx sancta Dialis ait:
' Donec ab Iliaca placidus purgamina Vesta
　' Detulerit flavis in mare Thybris aquis,
' Non mihi detonso crines depectere buxo,
　' Non ungues ferro subsecuisse licet: 230
' Non tetigisse virum, quamvis Iovis ille sacerdos,
　' Quamvis perpetua sit mihi lege datus.
' Tu quoque ne propera. melius tua filia nubet,
　' Ignea cum pura Vesta nitebit humo.'

　7 June.　Feast of the Fishers : Arctophylax sets.

Tertia post Nonas removere Lycaona Phoebe 235
　Fertur, et a tergo non habet Ursa metum.
Tunc ego me memini ludos in gramine Campi
　Aspicere et dici, lubrice Thybri, tuos.
Festa dies illis, qui lina madentia ducunt,
　Quique tegunt parvis aera recurva cibis. 240

　8 June.　Story of the Temple of Mens.

Mens quoque numen habet. Mentis delubra videmus
　Vota metu belli, perfide Poene, tui.
Poene rebellaras, et leto consulis omnes
　Attoniti Mauras pertimuere manus.
Spem metus expulerat, cum Menti vota senatus 245
　Suscipit. et melior protinus illa venit.
Aspicit instantes mediis sex lucibus Idus
　Illa dies, qua sunt vota soluta deae.

9 *June. Vesta's day. Account of her Temple, and its ceremonial.*

Vesta, fave! Tibi nunc operata resolvimus ora,
    Ad tua si nobis sacra venire licet.   250
In prece totus eram. caelestia numina sensi,
    Laetaque purpurea luce refulsit humus.
Non equidem vidi—valeant mendacia vatum—
    Te, dea: nec fueras aspicienda viro.
Sed quae nescieram, quorumque errore tenebar,   255
    Cognita sunt nullo praecipiente mihi.
Dena quater memorant habuisse Parilia Romam,
    Cum flammae custos aede recepta sua est:
Regis opus placidi, quo non metuentius ullum
    Numinis ingenium terra Sabina tulit.   260
Quae nunc aere vides, stipula tum tecta videres,
    Et paries lento vimine textus erat.
Hic locus exiguus, qui sustinet atria Vestae,
    Tunc erat intonsi regia magna Numae.
Forma tamen templi, quae nunc manet, ante fuisse   265
    Dicitur. et formae causa probanda subest.
Vesta eadem, quae Terra. subest vigil ignis utrique.
    Significantque deam tecta focusque suam.
Terra pilae similis, nullo fulcimine nixa,
    Aëre subiecto tam grave pendet onus.   270
Ipsa volubilitas libratum sustinet orbem,
    Quique premat partes, angulus omnis abest.
Cumque sit in media rerum regione locata,
    Et tangat nullum plusve minusve latus,
Ni convexa foret, parti vicinior esset,   275
    Nec medium terram mundus haberet onus.
Arte Syracosia suspensus in aëre clauso
    Stat globus, immensi parva figura poli:

Et quantum a summis, tantum secessit ab imis
   Terra. quod ut fiat, forma rotunda facit.   280
Par facies templi. nullus procurrit in illo
   Angulus. a pluvio vindicat imbre tholus.
Cur sit virginibus, quaeris, dea culta ministris?
   Inveniam causas hac quoque parte suas.
Ex Ope Iunonem memorant Cereremque creatas   285
   Semine Saturni. tertia Vesta fuit.
Utraque nupserunt, ambae peperisse feruntur:
   De tribus impatiens restitit una viri.
Quid mirum, virgo si virgine laeta ministra
   Admittit castas ad sua sacra manus?   290
Nec tu aliud Vestam, quam vivam intellege flammam:
   Nataque de flamma corpora nulla vides.
Iure igitur virgo est, quae semina nulla remittit,
   Nec capit, et comites virginitatis habet.
Esse diu stultus Vestae simulacra putavi: 295
   Mox didici curvo nulla subesse tholo.
Ignis inextinctus templo celatur in illo.
   Effigiem nullam Vesta nec ignis habet.
Stat vi terra sua. vi stando Vesta vocatur:
   Causaque par Grai nominis esse potest.   300
At focus a flammis et quod fovet omnia, dictus:
   Qui tamen in primis aedibus ante fuit.
Hinc quoque vestibulum dici reor. inde precando
   Praefamur Vestam, quae loca prima tenet.
Ante focos olim scamnis considere longis   305
   Mos erat, et mensae credere adesse deos.
Nunc quoque cum fiunt antiquae sacra Vacunae,
   Ante Vacunales stantque sedentque focos.
Venit in hos annos aliquid de more vetusto:
   Fert missos Vestae pura patella cibos.   310

The same day is also the Bakers' Festival.

Ecce coronatis panis dependet asellis,
    Et velant scabras florida serta molas.
Sola prius furnis torrebant farra coloni,
    Et Fornacali sunt sua sacra deae.
Suppositum cineri panem focus ipse parabat,   315
    Strataque erat tepido tegula quassa solo.
Inde focum servat pistor, dominamque focorum,
    Et quae pumiceas versat asella molas.
Praeteream, referamne tuum, rubicunde Priape,
    Dedecus? est multi fabula parva ioci.   320
Turrigera frontem Cybele redimita corona
    Convocat aeternos ad sua festa deos.
Convocat et satyros et, rustica numina, nymphas.
    Silenus, quamvis nemo vocarat, adest.
Nec licet, et longum est, epulas narrare deorum.   325
    In multo nox est pervigilata mero.
Hi temere errabant in opacae vallibus Idae:
    Pars iacet et molli gramine membra levat:
Hi ludunt: hos somnus habet: pars bracchia nectit,
    Et viridem celeri ter pede pulsat humum.   330
Vesta iacet, placidamque capit secura quietem,
    Sicut erat, positum cespite fulta caput.
At ruber hortorum custos nymphasque deasque
    Captat, et errantes fertque refertque pedes.
Aspicit et Vestam. dubium, nymphamne putarit,   335
    An scierit Vestam: scisse sed ipse negat.
Forte senex, quo vectus erat, Silenus asellum
    Liquerat ad ripas lene sonantis aquae.   340
Aggreditur divam longi deus Hellesponti,
    Intempestivo cum rudit ille sono.

Territa voce gravi surgit dea. convolat omnis
  Turba : per infestas effugit ille manus.
Lampsacos hoc animal solita est mactare Priapo : 345
  Apta asini flammis indicis exta damus.
Quem tu, diva, memor de pane monilibus ornas :
  Cessat opus, vacuae conticuere molae.

Story of Iuppiter Pistor.

Nomine, quam pretio, celebratior arce Tonantis,
  Dicam, Pistoris quid velit ara Iovis. 350
Cincta premebantur trucibus Capitolia Gallis :
  Fecerat obsidio iam diuturna famem.
Iuppiter, ad solium superis regale vocatis,
  'Incipe!' ait Marti. protinus ille refert :
'Scilicet ignotum est, quae sit fortuna meorum, 355
  'Et dolor hic animi voce querentis eget.
'Si tamen, ut referam breviter mala iuncta pudori,
  'Exigis : Alpino Roma sub hoste iacet.
'Haec est, cui fuerat promissa potentia rerum,
  'Iuppiter? hanc terris impositurus eras? 360
'Iamque suburbanos Etruscaque contudit arma.
  'Spes erat in cursu. nunc lare pulsa suo est.
'Vidimus ornatos aerata per atria picta
  'Veste triumphales occubuisse senes.
'Vidimus Iliacae transferri pignora Vestae 365
  'Sede. Putant aliquos scilicet esse deos!
'At si respicerent, qua vos habitatis in arce,
  'Totque domos vestras obsidione premi,
'Nil opis in cura scirent superesse deorum,
  'Et data sollicita tura perire manu. 370
'Atque utinam pugnae pateat locus! arma capessant,
  'Et, si non poterunt exsuperare, cadant.

'Nunc inopes victus, ignavaque fata timentes
  'Monte suo clausos barbara turba premit.'
Tunc Venus, et lituo pulcher trabeaque Quirinus,   375
  Vestaque pro Latio multa locuta suo est.
'Publica' respondit 'cura est pro moenibus istis,'
  Iuppiter 'et poenas Gallia victa dabit.
'Tu modo quae desunt fruges, superesse putentur,
  'Effice, nec sedes desere, Vesta, tuas.   380
'Quodcumque est solidae Cereris, cava machina frangat,
  'Mollitamque manu duret in igne focus.'
Iusserat, et fratris virgo Saturnia iussis
  Annuit. et mediae tempora noctis erant:
Iam ducibus somnum dederat labor. increpat illos   385
  Iuppiter. et sacro, quid velit, ore docet:
'Surgite, et in medios de summis arcibus hostes
  'Mittite, quam minime perdere vultis, opem!'
Somnus abit, quaeruntque novis ambagibus acti,
  Perdere quam nolint et iubeantur opem.   390
Esse Ceres visa est. iaciunt Cerialia dona:
  Iacta super galeas scutaque longa sonant.
Posse fame vinci spes excidit. Hoste repulso
  Candida Pistori ponitur ara Iovi.

Why the matrons walk barefoot on the Vestalia.

Forte revertebar festis Vestalibus illa,   395
  Quae Nova Romano nunc via iuncta foro est.
Huc pede matronam vidi descendere nudo:
  Obstipui, tacitus sustinuique gradum.
Sensit anus vicina loci, iussumque sedere
  Alloquitur, quatiens, voce tremente, caput: 400
'Hoc, ubi nunc fora sunt, udae tenuere paludes
  'Amne redundatis fossa madebat aquis.

'Curtius ille lacus, siccas qui sustinet aras,
  'Nunc solida est tellus, sed lacus ante fuit.
'Qua Velabra solent in Circum ducere pompas,   405
  'Nil praeter salices cassaque canna fuit.
'Saepe suburbanas rediens conviva per undas
  'Cantat, et ad nautas ebria verba iacit.
'Nondum conveniens diversis iste figuris
  'Nomen ab averso ceperat amne deus.   410
'Hic quoque lucus erat, iuncis et arundine densus
  'Et pede velato non adeunda palus.
'Stagna recesserunt et aquas sua ripa coercet,
  'Siccaque nunc tellus. mos tamen inde manet.'
Reddiderat causam. 'Valeas, anus optima!' dixi: 415
  'Quod superest aevi molle sit omne tui.'

*Story of the Palladium, and how Metellus saved it from the
fire of Vesta's Temple.*

Cetera iam pridem didici puerilibus annis,
  Non tamen idcirco praetereunda mihi.
Moenia Dardanides nuper nova fecerat Ilus:
  Ilus adhuc Asiae dives habebat opes: 420
Creditur armiferae signum caeleste Minervae
  Urbis in Iliacae desiluisse iuga.
Cura videre fuit. vidi templumque locumque.
  Hoc superest illic: Pallada Roma tenet.
Consulitur Smintheus, lucoque obscurus opaco   425
  Hos non mentito reddidit ore sonos:
Aetheream servate deam, servabitis Urbem:
  'Imperium secum transferet illa loci.'
Servat, et inclusam summa tenet Ilus in arce,
  Curaque ad heredem Laomedonta redit.   430
Sub Priamo servata parum. sic ipsa volebat,
  Ex quo iudicio forma revicta sua est.

Seu genus Adrasti, seu furtis aptus Ulixes,
    Seu pius Aeneas eripuisse datur.
Auctor in incerto : res est Romana. tuetur   435
    Vesta, quod assiduo lumine cuncta videt.
Heu quantum timuere patres, quo tempore Vesta
    Arsit, et est adytis obruta paene suis !
Flagrabant sancti sceleratis ignibus ignes,
    Mixtaque erat flammae flamma profana piae.   440
Attonitae flebant demisso crine ministrae :
    Abstulerat vires corporis ipse timor.
Provolat in medium, et magna 'Succurrite !' voce,
    'Non est auxilium flere' Metellus ait.
'Pignora virgineis fatalia tollite palmis !   445
    'Non ea sunt voto, sed rapienda manu !
'Me miserum ! dubitatis ?' ait. dubitare videbat,
    Et pavidas posito procubuisse genu.
Haurit aquas, tollensque manus, 'Ignoscite,' dixit
    'Sacra ! vir intrabo non adeunda viro.   450
'Si scelus est, in me commissi poena redundet :
    'Sit capitis damno Roma soluta mei.'
Dixit, et irrupit. factum dea rapta probavit,
    Pontificisque sui munere tuta fuit.
Nunc bene lucetis sacrae sub Caesare flammae :   455
    Ignis in Iliacis nunc erit estque focis.
Nullaque dicetur vittas temerasse sacerdos
    Hoc duce, nec viva defodietur humo.
Sic incesta perit, quia quam violavit, in illam
    Conditur, et Tellus Vestaque numen idem est.   460

Anniversary of Brutus' victory and Crassus' defeat.

Tum sibi Callaico Brutus cognomen ab hoste
    Fecit, et Hispanam sanguine tinxit humum.

Scilicet interdum miscentur tristia laetis,
  Nec populum toto pectore festa iuvant.
Crassus ad Euphraten aquilas natumque suosque   465
  Perdidit, et leto est ultimus ipse datus.
'Parthe, quid exultas?' dixit dea 'signa remittes:
'Quique necem Crassi vindicet, ultor erit.'

10 *June. Rising of the Dolphin.*

At simul auritis violae demuntur asellis,
  Et Cereris fruges aspera saxa terunt,   470
Navita puppe sedens 'Delphina videbimus,' inquit
  'Umida cum pulso nox erit orta die.'

11 *June. Matralia, and Festival of Matuta. Story of Ino.*

Iam, Phryx, a nupta quereris, Tithone, relinqui,
  Et vigil eois Lucifer exit aquis.
Ite, bonae matres,—vestrum Matralia festum—   475
  Flavaque Thebanae reddite liba deae.
Pontibus et magno iuncta est celeberrima Circo
  Area, quae posito de bove nomen habet.
Hac ibi luce ferunt Matutae sacra parenti
  Sceptriferas Servi templa dedisse manus.   480
Quae dea sit, quare famulas a limine templi
  Arceat—arcet enim—libaque tosta petat?
Bacche, racemiferos hedera redimite capillos,
  Si domus illa tua est, dirige vatis opus.
Arserat obsequio Semele Iovis. accipit Ino   485
  Te puer, et summa sedula nutrit ope.
Intumuit Iuno, raptum quod pelice natum
  Educet. at sanguis ille sororis erat.
Hinc agitur furiis Athamas et imagine falsa,
  Tuque cadis patria, parve Learche, manu.   490

Maesta Learcheas mater tumulaverat umbras,
  Et dederat miseris omnia iusta rogis.
Haec quoque, funestos ut erat laniata capillos,
  Prosilit, et cunis te, Melicerta, rapit.
Est spatio contracta brevi, freta bina repellit,   495
  Unaque pulsatur terra duabus aquis.
Huc venit insanis natum complexa lacertis,
  Et secum e celso mittit in alta iugo.
Excipit illaesos Panope centumque sorores,
  Et placido lapsu per sua regna ferunt.   500
Nondum Leucothea, nondum puer ille Palaemon,
  Verticibus densi Thybridis ora tenent.
Lucus erat. dubium Semelae, Stimulaene vocetur:
  Maenadas Ausonias incoluisse ferunt.
Quaerit ab his Ino, quae gens foret. Arcadas esse   505
  Audit, et Euandrum sceptra tenere loci.
Dissimulata deam Latias Saturnia bacchas
  Instimulat fictis insidiosa sonis:
'O nimium faciles, o toto pectore captae!
  'Non venit haec nostris hospes amica choris.   510
'Fraude petit, sacrique parat cognoscere ritum.
  'Quo possit poenas pendere, pignus habet.'
Vix bene desierat, complent ululatibus auras
  Thyiades, effusis per sua colla comis,
Iniciuntque manus, puerumque revellere pugnant.   515
  Quos ignorat adhuc, invocat illa deos:
'Dique virique loci, miserae succurrite matri!'
  Clamor Aventini saxa propinqua ferit.
Appulerat ripae vaccas Oetaeus Hiberas:
  Audit, et ad vocem concitus urget iter.   520
Herculis adventu, quae vim modo ferre parabant,
  Turpia femineae terga dedere fugae.

'Quid petis hinc,'—cognorat enim—'matertera Bacchi?
  'An numen quod me, te quoque vexat?' ait.
Illa docet partim, partim praesentia nati   525
  Continet, et furiis in scelus isse pudet.
Rumor, ut est velox, agitatis pervolat alis,
  Estque frequens, Ino, nomen in ore tuum.
Hospita Carmentis fidos intrasse penates
  Diceris, et longam deposuisse famem.   530
Liba sua properata manu Tegeaea sacerdos
  Traditur in subito cocta dedisse foco.
Nunc quoque liba iuvant festis Matralibus illam :
  Rustica sedulitas gratior arte fuit.
'Nunc,' ait 'o vates, venientia fata resigna,   535
  'Qua licet. hospitiis hoc, precor, adde meis.'
Parva mora est ; caelum vates ac numina sumit,
  Fitque sui toto pectore plena dei.
Vix illam subito posses cognoscere, tanto
  Sanctior et tanto, quam modo, maior erat.   540
'Laeta canam. gaude, defuncta laboribus Ino !'
  Dixit 'et huic populo prospera semper ades !
'Numen habes pelagi. natum quoque pontus habebit.
  'In vestris aliud sumite nomen aquis.
'Leucothea Grais, Matuta vocabere nostris :   545
  'In portus nato ius erit omne tuo.
'Quem nos Portunum, sua lingua Palaemona dicet.
  'Ite, precor, nostris aequus uterque locis !'
Annuerat. promissa fides. posuere labores :
  Nomina mutarunt. hic deus, illa dea est.   /   550

*Why no slaves admitted; and why the matrons bring not their
  own children.*

Cur vetet ancillas accedere, quaeritis ? Odit :
  Principiumque odii, si sinat illa, canam.

Una ministrarum solita est, Cadmeï, tuarum
  Saepe sub amplexus coniugis ire tui.
Improbus hanc Athamas furtim dilexit. ab illa   555
  Comperit agricolis semina tosta dari.
Ipsa quidem fecisse negas, sed fama recepit.
  Hoc est, cur odio sit tibi serva manus.
Non tamen hanc pro stirpe sua pia mater adoret.
  Ipsa parum felix visa fuisse parens.   560
Alterius prolem melius mandabitis illi.
  Utilior Baccho, quam fuit ipsa suis.

Anniversary of the death of Rutilius, 90, and Didius, 89.

Hanc tibi, 'Quo properas?' memorant dixisse, Rutili
  'Luce mea Marso consul ab hoste cades.'
Exitus accessit verbis, flumenque Toleni   565
  Purpureum mixtis sanguine fluxit aquis.
Proximus annus erat: Pallantide caesus eadem
  Didius hostiles ingeminavit opes.

*Festival of Temple of Fortune. Why the image of Servius is
  kept hidden with a toga.*

Lux eadem, Fortuna, tua est, auctorque, locusque.
  Sed superiniectis quis latet iste togis?   570
Servius est: iam constat enim. Sed causa latendi
  Discrepat, et dubium me quoque mentis habet.
Dum dea furtivos timide profitetur amores,
  Caelestemque homini concubuisse pudet,—
Arsit enim magno correpta cupidine regis,   575
  Caecaque in hoc uno non fuit illa viro—
Nocte domum parva solita est intrare fenestra:
  Unde Fenestellae nomina porta tenet.
Nunc pudet, et voltus velamine celat amatos,
  Oraque sunt multa regia tecta toga.   580

An magis est verum, post Tulli funera plebem
  Confusam placidi morte fuisse senis?
Nec modus ullus erat, crescebat imagine luctus,
  Donec eum positis occuluere togis.
Tertia causa mihi spatio maiore canenda est: 585
  Nos tamen adductos intus agemus equos.
Tullia coniugio, sceleris mercede, peracto
  His solita est dictis extimulare virum:
'Quid iuvat esse pares, te nostrae caede sororis,
  'Meque tui fratris, si pia vita placet?   590
'Vivere debuerant et vir meus et tua coniunx,
  'Si nullum ausuri maius eramus opus.
'Et caput et regnum facio dotale parentis.
  'Si vir es, i, dictas exige dotis opes!
'Regia res scelus est! socero cape regna necato,   595
  'Et nostras patrio sanguine tingue manus!'
Talibus instinctus solio privatus in alto
  Sederat. attonitum volgus ad arma ruit:
Hinc cruor, hinc caedes, infirmaque vincitur aetas:
  Sceptra gener socero rapta Superbus habet.   600
Ipse sub Esquiliis, ubi erat sua regia, caesus
  Concidit in dura sanguinulentus humo.
Filia carpento patrios initura penates,
  Ibat per medias alta feroxque vias.
Corpus ut aspexit, lacrimis auriga profusis   605
  Restitit. hunc tali corripit illa sono:
'Vadis, an expectas pretium pietatis amarum?
  'Duc, inquam, invitas ipsa per ora rotas!'
Certa fides facti. dictus Sceleratus ab illa
  Vicus, et aeterna res ea pressa nota.   610
Post tamen hoc ausa est templum, monimenta parentis,
  Tangere. mira quidem, sed tamen acta loquar.

Signum erat in solio residens sub imagine Tulli :
  Dicitur hoc oculis opposuisse manum.
Et vox audita est 'Voltus abscondite nostros,   615
  'Ne natae videant ora nefanda meae !'
Veste data tegitur. vetat hanc Fortuna moveri,
  Et sic e templo est ipsa locuta suo :
'Ore revelato qua primum luce patebit
  'Servius, haec positi prima pudoris erit.'   620
Parcite, matronae, vetitas attingere vestes :—
  Sollemni satis est voce movere preces :—
Sitque caput semper Romano tectus amictu,
  Qui rex in nostra septimus Urbe fuit.
Arserat hoc templum. signo tamen ille pepercit   625
  Ignis. opem nato Mulciber ipse tulit.
Namque pater Tulli Volcanus, Ocresia mater
  Praesignis facie Corniculana fuit.
Signa dedit genitor, tunc cum caput igne corusco   635
  Contigit, inque comis flammeus arsit apex.

*Festival of Temple of Concord, also on 11 June. Praise of
Caesar.*

Te quoque magnifica, Concordia, dedicat aede
  Livia, quam caro praestitit ipsa viro.
Disce tamen, veniens aetas, ubi Livia nunc est
  Porticus, immensae tecta fuisse domus.   640
Urbis opus domus una fuit, spatiumque tenebat,
  Quo brevius muris oppida multa tenent.
Haec aequata solo est, nullo sub crimine regni,
  Sed quia luxuria visa nocere sua.
Sustinuit tantas operum subvertere moles,   645
  Totque suas heres perdere Caesar opes.
Sic agitur censura et sic exempla parantur,
  Cum vindex, alios quod monet, ipse facit.

13 *June. The Ides. Account of the 'Quinquatrus minores' on
that day; the flute-players' procession, and ceremonial. (Minerva appears and instructs the poet.)*

Nulla nota est veniente die, quam discere possis.
   Idibus Invicto sunt data templa Iovi.   650
Et iam Quinquatrus iubeor narrare minores.
   Nunc ades o! coeptis, flava Minerva, meis.
'Cur vagus incedit tota tibicen in Urbe?
   'Quid sibi personae, quid stola longa volunt?'
Sic ego. Sic posita Tritonia cuspide dixit: 655
   Possim utinam doctae verba referre deae!
'Temporibus veterum tibicinis usus avorum
   'Magnus et in magno semper honore fuit.
'Cantabat fanis, cantabat tibia ludis,
   'Cantabat maestis tibia funeribus.   660
'Dulcis erat mercede labor. tempusque secutum,
   'Quod subito Graiae frangeret artis opus.
'Adde quod aedilis, pompam qui funeris irent,
   'Artifices solos iusserat esse decem.
'Exilio mutant Urbem, Tiburque recedunt.   665
   'Exilium quodam tempore Tibur erat!
'Quaeritur in scena cava tibia, quaeritur aris:
   'Ducit supremos nenia nulla toros.
'Servierat quidam, quantolibet ordine dignus,
   'Tibure. sed longo tempore liber erat.   670
'Rure dapes parat ille suo, turbamque canoram
   'Convocat. ad festas convenit illa dapes.
'Nox erat, et vinis oculique animique natabant,
   'Cum praecomposito nuntius ore venit.
'Atque ita, " Quid cessas convivia solvere?" dixit: 675
   '" Auctor vindictae iam venit ecce tuae."

'Nec mora, convivae valido titubantia vino
  'Membra movent. dubii stantque labantque pedes.
'At dominus "Discedite !" ait, plaustroque morantes
  'Sustulit. in plaustro scirpea lata fuit.   680
'Alliciunt somnos tempus, motusque, merumque,
  'Potaque se Tibur turba redire putat.
'Iamque per Esquilias Romanam intraverat urbem,
  'Et mane in medio plaustra fuere foro.
'Plautius, ut posset specie numeroque senatum   685
  'Fallere, personis imperat ora tegi,
'Admiscetque alios, et, ut hunc tibicina coetum
  'Augeat, in longis vestibus esse iubet :
'Sic reduces bene posse tegi, ne forte notentur
  'Contra collegae iussa redisse sui.   690
'Res placuit. cultuque novo libet Idibus uti,
  'Et canere ad veteres verba iocosa modos.'

*Why they are called Quinquatrus. Story of Minerva inventing
                    the flute.*

Haec ubi perdocuit, 'Superest mihi discere' dixi
  'Cur sit Quinquatrus illa vocata dies.'
'Martius' inquit 'agit tali mea nomine festa,   695
  'Estque sub inventis haec quoque turba meis.
'Prima, terebrato per rara foramina buxo,
  'Ut daret effeci tibia longa sonos.
'Vox placuit. faciem liquidis referentibus undis
  'Vidi virgineas intumuisse genas.   700
'"Ars mihi non tanti est. valeas, mea tibia !" dixi.
  'Excipit abiectam caespite ripa suo.
'Inventam Satyrus primum miratur, et usum
  'Nescit, et inflatam sensit habere sonum :

'Et modo dimittit digitis modo concipit auras: 705
   'Iamque inter nymphas arte superbus erat.
'Provocat et Phoebum. Phoebo superante pependit:
   'Caesa recesserunt a cute membra sua.
'Sum tamen inventrix auctorque ego carminis huius.
   'Hoc est, cur nostros ars colat ista dies.'   710

15 *June.   Hyades rise: Vesta's temple cleansed.*

Tertia lux veniet, qua tu, Dodoni Thyene,
   Stabis Agenorei fronte videnda bovis.
Haec est illa dies, qua tu purgamina Vestae,
   Thybri, per Etruscas in mare mittis aquas.
Si qua fides ventis, zephyro date carbasa, nautae!   715
   Cras veniet vestris ille secundus aquis.

16 *June.   Evening rising of Orion.*

At pater Heliadum radios ubi tinxerit undis,
   Et cinget geminos stella serena polos,
Tollet humo validos proles Hyriea lacertos.

17 *June.   Dolphin rises at night.   Anniversary of Tubertus'
           victory over Aequi and Volsci.*

Continua Delphin nocte videndus erit.   720
Scilicet hic olim Volscos Aequosque fugatos
   Viderat in campis, Algida terra, tuis:
Unde suburbano clarus, Tuberte, triumpho,
   Vectus es in niveis, Postume, victor equis.

19 *June.*   *Sun passes to the Crab.*   *Festival of Minerva on the Aventine.*

Iam sex et totidem luces de mense supersunt,   725
    Huic unum numero tu tamen adde diem.
Sol abit a Geminis, et Cancri signa rubescunt:
    Coepit Aventina Pallas in arce coli.

20 *June.*   *Festival of Summanus.*   *Story of Aesculapius.*

Iam tua, Laomedon, oritur nurus, ortaque noctem
    Pellit, et e pratis uda pruina fugit: 730
Reddita, quisquis is est, Summano templa feruntur,
    Tum, cum Romanis, Pyrrhe, timendus eras.
Hanc quoque cum patriis Galatea receperit undis,
    Plenaque securae terra quietis erit,
Surgit humo iuvenis telis afflatus avitis,   735
    Et geminas nexo porrigit angue manus.
Notus amor Phaedrae, nota est iniuria Thesei:
    Devovit natum credulus ille suum.
Non impune pius iuvenis Troezena petebat:
    Dividit obstantes pectore taurus aquas.   740
Solliciti terrentur equi, frustraque retenti
    Per scopulos dominum duraque saxa trahunt.
Exciderat curru, lorisque morantibus artus
    Hippolytus lacero corpore raptus erat,
Reddideratque animam, multum indignante Diana.   745
    'Nulla' Coronides 'causa doloris' ait:
'Namque pio iuveni vitam sine volnere reddam,
    'Et cedent arti tristia fata meae.'
Gramina continuo loculis depromit eburnis:—
    Profuerant Glauci manibus illa prius,   750
Tunc, cum observatas anguis descendit in umbras,
    Usus et auxilio est augur ab angue dato:—

Pectora ter tetigit, ter verba salubria dixit:
　　Depositum terra sustulit ille caput.
Lucus eum nemorisque tui, Dictynna, recessus　　755
　　Celat: Aricino Virbius ille lacu.
At Clymenus Clothoque dolent: haec, fila reneri,
　　Hic, fieri regni iura minora sui.
Iuppiter, exemplum veritus, direxit in ipsum
　　Fulmina, qui nimiae moverat artis opem.　　760
Phoebe, querebaris. deus est, placare parenti:
　　Propter te, fieri quod vetat, ipse facit.

　　23 *June. Anniversary of the defeat of Thrasymene.*

Non ego te, quamvis properabis vincere, Caesar,
　　Si vetet auspicium, signa movere velim.
Sint tibi Flaminius Trasimenaque litora testes,　　765
　　Per volucres aequos multa monere deos.
Tempora si veteris quaeris temeraria damni,
　　Quartus ab extremo mense bis ille dies.

24 *June. Anniversary of defeat of Syphax, and of victory
　　of the Metaurus. Feast of Fors Fortuna.*

Postera lux melior. superat Masinissa Syphacem,
　　Et cecidit telis Hasdrubal ipse suis.　　770
Tempora labuntur, tacitisque senescimus annis,
　　Et fugiunt freno non remorante dies.
Quam cito venerunt Fortunae Fortis honores!
　　Post septem luces Iunius actus erit.
Ite, deam laeti Fortem celebrate, Quirites!　　775
　　In Tiberis ripa munera regis habet.
Pars pede, pars etiam celeri decurrite cumba.
　　Nec pudeat potos inde redire domum.
Ferte coronatae iuvenum convivia lintres,
　　Multaque per medias vina bibantur aquas.　　780

Plebs colit hanc, quia, qui posuit, de plebe fuisse
    Fertur, et ex humili sceptra tulisse loco.
Convenit et servis, serva quia Tullius ortus
    Constituit dubiae templa propinqua deae.

26 June.   Rising of belt of Orion: and the solstice.

Ecce suburbana rediens male sobrius aede   785
    Ad stellas aliquis talia verba iacit:
'Zona latet tua nunc, et cras fortasse latebit:
    'Dehinc erit, Orion, aspicienda mihi.'
At si non esset potus, dixisset eadem
    Venturum tempus solstitiale die.   790

27 June.   Festival of the Larum Sacellum, and Temple of Iuppiter Stator.

Lucifero subeunte Lares delubra tulerunt
    Hic, ubi fit docta multa corona manu.
Tempus idem Stator aedis habet, quam Romulus olim
    Ante Palatini condidit ora iugi.

29.   Festival of the Temple of Quirinus.

Tot restant de mense dies, quot nomina Parcis,   795
    Cum data sunt trabeae templa, Quirine, tuae.

30 June.   Festival of the Temple of Hercules and the Muses. Clio appears and gives the poet an account of it.

Tempus Iuleis cras est natale Kalendis:
    Pierides, coeptis addite summa meis.
Dicite, Pierides, quis vos adiunxerit isti,
    Cui dedit invitas victa noverca manus?   800
Sic ego. sic Clio: 'Clari monimenta Philippi
    'Aspicis, unde trahit Marcia casta genus:

'Marcia, sacrifico deductum nomen ab Anco,
  'In qua par facies nobilitate sua,
'Par animo quoque forma suo respondet. in illa   805
  'Et genus et facies ingeniumque simul.
'Nec quod laudamus formam, tu turpe putaris.
  'Laudamus magnas hac quoque parte deas.
'Nupta fuit quondam matertera Caesaris illi.
  'O decus, o sacra femina digna domo!'   810
Sic cecinit Clio.   doctae assensere sorores:
  Annuit Alcides increpuitque lyram.

NOTES.

Page 19.

[1—100. (Explanations of the name *Iunius* for the month.)

Poets are inspired (5—8): in a thick wood *Iuno* appeared to me (9—20): she says: 'June is called after me, and I am worthy the honour; else I should repent the favour shewn to the Romans' (21—64). Hebe replied: 'I plead for my sole honour; the month is called after *iuvenes*. Romulus divided the people into elders, and younger men' (65—88). Then appeared Concord, and proclaimed that June was derived from 'iunctus' in memory of the *union* of Sabines and Romans. I do not decide between goddesses (89—100).]

1. *in nomine*, 'in the matter of its name' lit.; i. e. · diverse sources for its name'.

2. *placeant*, indirect quest.   See Scheme of Moods.
leges, 'choose'.

3. *erunt qui loquantur*, 'there will be those who say'.   In this kind of phrase the subord. verb is always subjunctive, because the meaning is *consecutive;* 'there will be people *such as to* say', 'people of *the kind to* say'.   See Scheme.

5. The divine inspiration or 'stirring' (*impetus*) of the poet (as Ovid gives it) has lost all illusion: it is become a mere conventional artifice of poetry.

6. 'has the seeds of the inspired mind'; i. e. this possession by the god brings the divine power of the poet.

10. *si non obstreperetur aquis*, 'were it not that the waters plash'. When the imperfect is used in conditionals, it is always of a supposition *excluded by the fact ;* so here: the waters do plash.

12. *in cura eram*, 'was wrapped in thought'.

13. Hesiod, born at Ascra in Boeotia (N. Greece), from being a shepherd (*oves*) became the first great poet of agriculture: his poem

Works and Days is still extant. He falls somewhere in the 8th
century B.C.

15—16. *contulit*, 'compared'. The reference is to the famous
judgment of Paris. He was son of Priam, king of Troy: and when at
a banquet of the gods an apple inscribed 'to the fairest' had been
thrown in by Eris (strife), and the three goddesses Here, Athena,
and Aphrodite (see list of gods) could not agree which was to have
it: they referred the decision to Paris, who decided for Aphrodite.
Hence came the troubles of the Trojan war, ending in the sack of
Troy, 100. The whole story is told by Tennyson in *Oenone*.

Ida is the mountain in the Troad (N. W. Asia Minor) at the foot of
which Troy lay.

una fuit, Iuno (Here): she was the sister and wife of Iuppiter, and
queen of gods.

Cf. 'divom incedo regina Iovisque et soror et coniunx.'

Verg. *Ae.* I. 46.

18. *arce Iovis.* The Capitol at Rome has two summits, and when
both are mentioned they are regularly called *Arx Capitoliumque*, the
former (prob.) lying N.E., and the latter W. But often, as here, *either
name* is used for *both* summits. In this temple of Iuppiter, which was
on the Capitol proper, there were three chapels or cells, one for Iuppiter
in the centre, and Minerva and Iuno on the right and left. The old and
famous temple had been burnt 82 B.C., but restored magnificently
by Sulla and (on Sulla's death) Lutatius Catulus: the later building was
apparently gilt, prob. in the roof, 73.

19. *animum*, 'feeling', i.e. 'fear'.

Page 20.

21. *conditor*, 'poet': *condere* prop. 'to put together', regularly
used of writing verses, and then even w. acc. 'to sing of' as v. 24.

25. *traharis*, 'be led astray', as Ovid had been; for I. 41 he says:
'iuvenum de nomine quartus'; 'the fourth month (June, by old reckoning) is called from the name of *iuvenes*': so below 65 sqq.

28. *dubito glorier*, 'I doubt whether to be more proud' (indirect
deliberative, see Scheme). With the full construction it would be *num
glorier*, but *num* is easily and often omitted.

30. *sors*, i.e. 'offspring'. To call a child a *sors* 'gift of fate', 'lot'
is not unnatural in the case of men, but rather fanciful as applied to
gods.

32. *a caelo: prope* is often used with *ab:* we only use 'from' after 'far', not after 'near'.

33. *torus*, prop. 'couch', hence 'marriage': 'if 'tis marriage you value' in giving honour, in estimating my rank.

34. *Tarpeio*, the precipice on the S.W. side of the Capitol was the Tarpeian rock, and the name was often given to the whole of that summit: the other summit being properly the arx, though both Arx and Capitolium are often used loosely (e.g. 18) for the whole hill with both its summits.

35. *pelex*, 'a concubine'. Maia, the mother of Mercury by Iuppiter. The jealous Iuno is a familiar figure both in the *Iliad* and *Aeneid.*

36. *invidiosus*, 'resented'. She means 'shall not I be allowed who have the better right?'

39. *luces*, 'the new moons'; plural because of the recurrence.

Lucina, the goddess of 'light' (as here) and birth (invoked by women in childbirth), was sometimes identified with Iuno (so *Fasti* II. 435) and sometimes with Diana (Hor. *Car. Sec.* 15 'sive tu Lucina probas vocari' of Diana).

40. *a nullo nomina mense traham*, 'draw my title from no month', a rather perverse inversion of her real meaning '*give* my name to no month'.

41. *paeniteat*, 'let me repent'. Jussive: a better and more forcible meaning than taking it condit. 'I should repent'.

posuisse, as often, 'laid down'.

42. *genus Electrae.* Electra was the mother of Dardanus, the mythical founder of the Trojan race. Iuno hated the Trojans and favoured the Greeks in consequence of the judgment of Paris (*Idaeo iudice*, 44).

43. *Ganymedes*, a beautiful boy whom the eagle of Iuppiter bore off to heaven to be Jove's cup-bearer. Iuno resented the favour shewn to him. He was a son of the royal house of Troy, and was 'rapt from Ida': and so increased Iuno's hatred against the race.

44. *Idaeo iudice*, not 'by' him, which would be *ab:* but abl. abs., lit. 'the Idaean being judge', i.e. 'by the award of the Idaean'. Horace is especially fond of such absolutes: 'scriberis Vario...alite', *Od.* I. 6. 1, 'iudice laudatus Caesare', *Sat.* II. 1. 84, 'curatus inaequali tonsore', *Ep.* I. 1. 94. See below, 283.

45. *Carthaginis.* Verg. *Aen.* I. says: 'Iuno loved Carthage more than all lands save Samos, and there were her arms and car, there she

plotted, did fate allow, the empire of the world should be'. This line
expresses a regret that she had transferred her favour to Rome.

47. Sparta, Argos and Mycenae, ancient cities of Peloponnesus
(S. Greece), were famed as under the special charge of Iuno: so was
Samos (isle of Aegean). See 45.

49. The Sabines, acc. to the old story, under king Tatius, made
war upon the Romans, who had carried off their maidens for wives.
These women interceded between the two armies, and they dwelt together after that as one people at Rome.

Iuno was worshipped both by them and by the Falisci, people of
Etruscan town of Falerii, as Iuno Quiritis or the Spear-bearer.

50. *tuli*, 'bore', i.e. 'allowed'.

Page 21.

53. *Mavors*, Mamers, Mars, are various forms of the name of the
Latin god of war. He was an especial object of worship at Rome, and
was represented as the father of Romulus (the founder of the city according to the tale). Mars being the son of Iuno, Romulus was her 'nepos'
or grandson.

55. *fides*, prop. 'faith', often used as here by a transference of
meaning for 'fulfilment'.

58. *suburbani*, 'the neighbours', i.e. the cities near, as the context
shews.

59. *Aricia*, on the Appian way, just near the Alban hills.

60. *Laurentum*, old Latin town, S.W. of Rome, near the sea.

Lanuvium, another old Latin town a little farther on the Appian
way from Rome.

61. *Tibur*, on the upper Anio, on the edge of the Appennines, a
few miles E. of Rome.

62. *Praeneste*, a little S. of Tibur, in a fine position in a gap of the
hills.

63. *tempus*, 'season', i.e. 'month'.

65. *Herculis uxor* was Hebe, daughter of Iuppiter and Iuno, and
goddess of Youth: so the point is, that she too claims the month as
called after the Young (iuniores).

70. *partes ago*, exactly as we say, 'act the part'.

71. *mei iuris tenuisse*, lit. 'to keep it as part of my right', i.e. 'keep
it in my power'.

malim, potential, 'I should prefer'.

72. *faveas*, subj. common with *forsitan*, 'perchance you may'.

73. *possedit*, 'has occupied' (possĭdēre). *socio* is explained by 18. See note.

75. *origine*, abl. of cause, 'from the month's origin', i.e. from the fact that the month draws its name from *iuniores*.

79. *nomine*, 'on account of', 'for sake of': a not uncommon use in Latin, thus, 'tuo nomine gratulabantur', 'on your account', Cic. *Phil.* I. 12. 30. The metaphor is very probably (like ours) from money dealings, as 'nomen' is a person's *name* or *account* in the creditor's books.

80. The allusion is to the story of Cacus and Hercules, told I. 543, Verg. *Aen.* VIII. 185. Cacus, son of the fire-god Vulcan (which explains 81), was a monster who lived in a cave on the Aventine hill at Rome. Hercules came that way, with the oxen of the three-headed Geryon; and Cacus, while he was asleep, stole his cattle, dragging them by their tails into the cave. The lowing of the oxen betrayed the theft, and Hercules chased C. into his cave, tore it open and slew him in spite of his fiery breath. The splendid passage in Vergil should be read.

Page 22.

81. Vulcan, his father, gave him fiery breath.

83. *digessit ab annis*, 'divided by their years', i.e. into older and younger. The ages, according to the Servian arrangement, were 17—46 for the younger, 46 upwards for the older.

88. *senum*, i.e. *Maius* from *maiores*. The fuller account, v. 55.

90. *pietas*, 'love' of kindred, being so sacred: regular meaning. Thus Aeneas from his goodness towards his father (as well as the gods) is called *pius* always in the *Aeneid*.

91. *Concordia*. One of the most famous temples at Rome (at N.W. end of forum) was dedicated to Harmony, in 367 B.C., when the patricians and plebeians were 'reconciled' by the Licinian laws, admitting plebs to the consulship. Augustus had restored 'harmony' all over the empire, as his triumph had brought to an end the century of civil wars and troubles. So she is fairly called the 'Spirit and Work of the Peaceful Ruler', 92.

92. *nexa comas*, common poetical construction for *nexis comis*, 'her hair twined'. The construction is remarkable, as the accusative is retained, though the verb is passive. It is probably an imitation of Greek, some of the instances resembling the Greek *passive* use (ἐπιτετραμμένος τὴν ἀρχήν 'entrusted with the rule') and some the *middle* (προβεβλημένος

τὴν ἀσπίδα, 'having cast his shield before him'); but the Romans would imitate both without distinguishing.

Compare *caput detectus honestum*, Verg. *A.* x. 133; *suspensi loculos lacerto*, 'their satchels hung on their arm', Hor. *S.* i. 6. 74.

It is chiefly found in the Augustan poets, and there it is common.

93. Cf. 49.

94. *suis* refers to *regna*.

95. *lares,* the old Latin gods of the household, who were worshipped on all family occasions, and regularly had their plate at the family meal, and were crowned on great days. The united Rome is here pictured as under one common lar.

99. *pares,* 'equal' in honour: he won't decide. *iudice* abl. of cause.

100. *Pergama* (Greek word 'the stronghold'), old name of Troy.
iuvet, 'would benefit', potential.

[100—182. 1 June. Festival of Carna. The tale is told, how the nymph became a huntress (105—112), eluded all lovers (113—118), till Ianus at last seizes her (119—126). With the thorn that he gives her she drives the bloodsucking screech-owls from the house of Alban Proca (129—168). The origin of the special custom of eating bacon, beans and meal on this day (169—182).]

101. Ovid represents the goddess of the 'hinge' (Cardea from *cardo*) and the goddess of the healthy body (Carna, from *cor*, or better *caro*, 'flesh') as the same. Others make them different.

Page 23.

108. *procis,* 'suitors' [prec-]. The dative is used by Augustan writers after the passive participle, in imitation of the Greek construction (τὰ ἐμοὶ πεπραγμένα, 'the things done *by* me').

109. *sequi,* 'to scour', 'hunt', a slight stretch of meaning: what she really *hunts* is the game, of course.

113. *dixisset.* It is natural, instead of saying '*If* he had spoken, she replied', to say more forcibly, 'Let him have said...she replied'. In this way the jussive subjunctive is easily used for the regular conditional.

117. *ut,* 'when', always has indic.
resistit, 'stops short', the duped lover being in front: when he turns to find her, she has disappeared.

119. *Ianus*, the god of 'opening'. The most ancient gateways were two archways and a chamber between them, open at both ends: so the god was represented with two faces, fore and aft. The old tradition of opening his temple in time of war and closing it in peace probably originally meant that he was invoked to bless the army marching out to war.

120. *ad*, not simply 'to', which would be dat., but 'to assail her'.

123. *gerantur*, indirect quest., 2.

125. *occupat*, 'seizes'.

 munus cardinis, 'the office of the hinge'.

129. *spina*, 'the white thorn'. *tristes noxas*, 'evil mischief': i.e. all sorts of horrors and plagues.

Observe the position of the parenthesis: Ov. shews great ingenuity in overcoming the difficulty of the metre without destroying the simplicity of the narrative.

131. *Phineus* (adj. Phineïus) was a Thracian king who for his cruelty to his sons, on false suspicion, was punished by having all his food either snatched from him or defiled by hideous winged monsters called Harpies (Harpyiae). The best description of these beasts is Verg. *Aen.* III. 225.

133. *stantes*, 'staring'; the notion is '*fixed*', and the word 'stare' is from the same stem.

135. *egentes*, 'in want of' [in many good Latin writers with *gen.* (Hor. Caes., &c.), though Cic. has it with abl. usually], he means not 'without a nurse', but 'so young as to need a nurse', 'nurslings'.

136. *vitiant*, lit. 'spoil', so 'devour', 'rend'.

Page 24.

137. *lactentia viscera* (rather unusual words), 'their tender flesh'.

139. 'Their name is Screech-owls'. The dat. *strigibus* attracted to agree with *illis*, according to the regular use in this formula of names: the predicate is dat. as well as the person.

140. *horrendum*, Bentley's emendation for MSS. *horrenda*.

 stridere. The name is a Greek name στρίξ, and of course is not formed from *strideo*, but from the Greek stem στριγ- 'screech', word made from sound. The etymologies of the ancients were mere guesses; and indeed as strid- and στριγ- are connected, this is nearer than usual. See 299.

Observe *stridĕre, e* short. This is the old form of the verb, and survives in poetry, where it is convenient: thus we find fervĕre, tergĕre, fulgĕre, &c. The perfects vidi, sedi, movi, &c., are evidences of the same fact in other verbs where the short present exists no longer.

141.   *carmine,* 'by a charm'. The Marsian or Sabine women were reputed great in spells and incantations. Compare Horace's three famous poems about the witch Canidia (*Epod.* V. XVII., *Sat.* I. viii), where he professes to believe 'caputque Marsa dissilire nenia', 'the head is torn asunder with the Marsian spell'.

142.   Sense: 'whether they are really birds, or hags changed by witchcraft'.

143.   *Proca,* one of the fabulous kings of Alba Longa.

in illis quinque diebus, the regular idiom for 'within the last five days', 'within five days from then': so 'hoc biennio' (Cic. *Scip. Som.* 2) 'within two years from now'.

146.   *vagit,* 'cries': from the sound (wa !).

149.   *quid faceret?* 'what was she to do?' This is the past deliberative.   *quid faciam?* 'what am I to do?' is the primary deliberative (the subjunctive being really the jussive put as a question, *facias,* 'you must do': '*quid faciam,* 'what must I do?'): it is found in the past form, commonly when indirect (*nesciebat quid faceret,* 'he did not know what to do') and rarely direct, as here, when the past embarrassment is put dramatically.

olim (from *olle,* old form of *ille*) prop. 'at that time'. So used both past and future: and often, as here, of imaginary cases, in similes. We should say 'ofttimes'.   [-im is old locative termination, and appears in enim, raptim, hinc, &c.]

155.   *arbutea.* The arbutus or strawberry-tree (found in many gardens in S. England) is common in Italy.

156.   *notat,* 'marks', 'makes signs'.

158.   *cruda* [prop. 'hard', cf. *crustum,* κρύ-ος, κρύσταλλον], 'raw'.

bimenstre, with -ĕ for the regular ī, a bye-form adopted no doubt for its convenience. The complex rules in the grammar for the third declension of nouns (and the corresponding adjectives) shew the constant tendency to corrupt ī into ĕ. So *perenne,* III. 654.

161.   *fibra,* prop. 'thread' [fid- 'to split']', so 'entrail'.

164.   *assint,* subj. because the sentence is orat. obliq. after *vetat.*

165.   *Ianalis,* 129.

Page 25.

169. *larda* (prop. adj.), 'bacon'.

172. *ascitas*, lit. 'fetched in', so 'foreign'. The luxurious tendency of the wealthy Romans, which reached such a height in the first century of the empire, was already fatally apparent.

173. *fraude*, 'harm', its older meaning.

Fish was a great article of luxury in the empire. Juvenal (*S.* IV.) has a famous mock-heroic account of a huge turbot caught in Domitian's reign, which required a privy council to consider how to dispose and serve it up.

Oysters, too, were a great delicacy. In the same satire (140) we read of a man who could tell at the first taste whether an oyster came from Latium, Campania, or Britain.

175. The Ionian bird is the *attagen*, said to be the 'god-wit' (a longbilled wader).

176. The Pygmies (πυγμαῖοι, πυγ-, 'men as big as a fist', Tom-Thumbs) were a fabulous dwarf-race, of whom Homer tells us (*Il.* III. 5) that they lived on Oceanus (the water at the edge of the earth), and were warred upon by the cranes; so this bird is the crane.

177. For afterwards his flesh 'pleased' them.

178. The MSS. reading here is '*miserat ante feras*', which is clearly corrupt: for as it stands it can only mean 'the earth had till then not given them snared game', which is rather flat, where one expects the mention of some special delicacy. Merkel's reading *arte* is an improvement: the meaning being that the capture of game had not yet become a regular skilled labour.

181. *sextis Kalendis*, on this day, 1 June, being the kalends of the sixth month.

[183—196. 1 June, also the festival of Iuno Moneta on the Arx. It stood where the house of Manlius had been (183—186): happy had he died when he saved the Capitol (187—190). Also the festival of Mars' temple near Capena gate, and Tempestas (191—196).]

183. Temple of Iuno Moneta, vowed by F. Camillus (345 B.C.), acc. to Livy (VII. 28), because 'he wanted the aid of the gods' in a battle with the Aurunci. Moneta means the 'adviser' [moneo]. It afterwards became the coining-establishment at Rome, and thus, curiously enough, is the origin of the words 'mint' and 'money'.

185. M. Manlius, besieged with the Romans in the Capitol by the Gauls (390 B.C.), was awoke (according to the famous story) by the

cackling of some geese to find the Gauls just scaling the citadel: he hastily roused his comrades and drove them back.

In 384 Manlius, having espoused the cause of the poor and oppressed plebeians, was virulently attacked by the patricians; the cry of aspiring to be king was successfully raised, and he was convicted of treason and executed by being hurled from the Tarpeian cliff of the Capitol. Thus as Livy (VI. 20) says, 'the same place was the monument of his signal glory and his death'.

190. 'This name (i. e. of a traitor, aspiring to kingdom) his long life gave him': for if he had died young he would have only been known as the saviour of Rome. (Ovid seems to forget how soon after it was.)

192. The Porta Capena was a gate in the old Servian wall, just below the Caelian hill. Not far from here there was a cloister (tecta via) to the temple of Mars. This was the temple from which on the Ides of Quintilis (15 July) the knights rode to the Capitol, in memory of Regillus (see Macaulay's Lays: 'but the proud Ides when the squadron rides shall be Rome's brightest day': again, 'from Castor in the forum to Mars without the wall': also Liv. IX. 46). The first of June is the Commemoration-day of this temple, and that of Tempestas, below.

193. *Tempestas,* said to be a temple near the Capena gate, and vowed after the successes of Lucius Cornelius Scipio (260 B.C.) in Corsica. This was in the beginning of the first Punic War, when the Romans first took to the naval service: and it was natural that a special temple of Tempestas should then be wanted. The Mediterranean has very violent squalls.

196. 'The taloned bird of Jove' is of course the eagle. The reference here is to the constellation of the Eagle, which rose at sunset on the first of June.

The difficulties of the ancient astronomy are several. See Introduction, *On the Astronomy of Ovid.*

Page 26.

[197—199 June 2. The Hyades rise.]

197. Hyades [ὕω, 'to rain'], so called because they were supposed to bring wet weather: but this was probably connected rather with their morning setting than their morning rising, as the former was in November.

Taurinae. The large constellation called the Bull (one of the Zodiac signs) contained the Hyades in its forehead.

[199—208. 3 June. Festival of temple of Bellona : the origin of
it ; its ancient pillar]

199. *mane ubi bis fuerit,* 'when it has twice dawned': *mane* still
an adv.

201. Bellona, the goddess of war, had a temple in the Circus Flaminius (just. N. of the Capitol). It was vowed by Appius Claudius
the Blind (the great Censor, who built a great aqueduct and began the
Appian way), in a fight with the Etruscans. Liv. X. 19.

duello, original form of 'bello' (the v sound being hardened, and d
disappearing). Cf. bis=duis.

203. This refers to the famous scene in the senate, when Pyrrhus
(king of Epirus) had beaten the Romans at Heraclea (280 B.C.) on the
Tarentine gulf, and sent the eloquent Cineas to Rome to offer peace.
The Senate was about to accept it, when the blind old Appius Claudius
was carried in a litter to the house, and delivered such a speech that the
peace was unanimously rejected. Arnold compares the great scene in
the House of Lords on 7 April, 1788, when Chatham delivered his dying
speech against peace with America.

auctor of the temple.

pace negata, poetical use of the participle, without any idea of its
being past ' in the refusal of peace '.

204. *captus* ' seized ', and so by a transference of use ' robbed ', with
the abl. of depriving.

205. *summum,* 'the top' where the races started.

206. *notae* 'of mark ', as we say (gen. quality).

207. The ancient custom of declaring war was to hurl a spear across
the enemy's frontier. When the Roman conquests were so large as
to make this inconvenient, the custom was kept up, but by a legal fiction
the pillar near the temple of Bellona was regarded as the frontier and
the spear thrown thence. The instinct to retain old ceremonies, even
when the old meaning had become lost or modified, was very strong
with the Romans. The pillar was called Columna Bellica, and the
Fetialis was the official who threw the spear.

[209—212. 4 June : Festival of temple of Hercules Custos.]

209. In another part of the Circus Flaminius (prob. the W. end)
was the temple of Hercules the Guardian (Custos). It appears from this
passage that the temple was built in obedience to a Sibylline oracle (see
next line), and the building (at least in the shape as Ovid knew it) was
superintended by Sulla, presumably while dictator (82—79).

210. The Sibylline books were sacred oracles, written in Greek,

and probably from the old Euboean colony of Cumae in Campania (hence called Cumaean, or, as here, *Euboicus*) : the old story was that the Sibyl herself offered nine books for sale to king Tarquin ; being refused, she burnt three, offering the rest for the same price. After a second refusal she came back again, having burnt three more, and the remaining three were purchased for the original sum. They were kept strictly secret, and were consulted in time of trouble by order of the Senate. When the temple of Iuppiter was burnt in 82 (cf. 18), a new Sibylline collection was made and kept in the restored temple.

quod munus, 'this honour' of being enshrined here.

211. 'The time of the honour (i. e. festival of the temple) is the day before the nones'.

Lucifer, the morning star, often used for 'dawn' or 'day'. See 474.

The *nones* were the 9th day (or 8th, as they counted *inclusively*, and we do not) before the Ides, which were on 13th; excepting March, July, October, when they were on 15th. Thus the Ides of June are 13th, nones 5th, and this day 4th.

212. *titulum,* 'a name', i. e. of the founder.

probare was the word used of the Censor who superintended the building, and said that the builder did his work properly : if so, the Censor 'approved', and his name 'titulus' was inscribed on it.

The autocrat Sulla performed this office himself.

[213—218. 5 June : Nones. Festival of the Temple of Semo, Sancus, or Fidius.]

213. Semo, Sancus, or Dius Fidius [clearly 'the god of Faith or Honour', from *fides* or *sancio*] was a very ancient Sabine deity, whose temple was on the N. W. edge of the Quirinal hill. It contained many old relics, and among others a wooden shield covered with oxhide, on which was written in old characters a treaty between Tarquin the Proud and Gabii.

Fidio-ne. In prose we should have *ne, num,* or *utrum* with the first word, *an* with the second : in poetry we often find *ne* alone with the second.

referrem, indirect delib. Cf. 28, and Scheme.

215. *istis: iste,* always used with reference to second person, 'that of yours' : so here 'those you name'.

216. *Cures,* old Sabine town about 20 miles N. of Rome.

[219—234. Digression. The poet is advised by the wife of the Priest of Iuppiter not to celebrate his daughter's marriage before the Ides of June.]

This digression is probably introduced here because on June 7 the cleansing of the Temple was begun.

220. *qua sospite,* abl. abs.

Page 27.

221. *taedis,* frequent, for the 'marriage-torch' which conducted the bride to her new home.

222. *forent,* subj., indirect question.

223. *sacras,* for all Ides were sacred to Iuppiter, as he tells us, I. 56, 'Idibus alba Iovi grandior agna cadit'.

225. *huius,* June.

thalamis aliena, 'unfit for marriage'.

226. The priest of Iuppiter was called *flamen Dialis* [Di-alis, stem DIV- 'bright', corrupted DIOV-, cf. Δι-ός]: the marriage of a flamen was indissoluble (232), and if his wife died he had to resign his office. His life was one mass of quaint privileges, and still more quaint restrictions, which here seem to apply to his wife too (229—230).

227. On the 15th June the Temple of Vesta was cleaned out, and the dirt carried away behind the building. It was an extremely unpropitious day until this was done, but propitious afterwards. See Introduction, § 5, III.

Vesta is called *Iliaca,* because according to the tradition Aeneas, after the siege of Troy, brought the fires of Vesta to Rome. The Greeks called her Ἑστία, 'the hearth' [VAS- 'dwell'], and the Roman name is the same. She was the 'family-goddess' of the nation, and in her temple was the Eternal hearth-fire in place of statue: hence '*Ignea*', 234.

229. These seemingly absurd rules doubtless meant that on so unpropitious a day not even the most trifling thing was to be begun by so sacred a person.

232. *perpetua lege datus,* 'bound to me for ever' as divorce was impossible (226).

[235—240. 7 June: Festival of the Fishers, in honour of Tiber.]

235. A couplet difficult from its allusiveness.

'The 3rd night after the nones (7 June by Roman reckoning) is said to draw off Lycaon, and the Bear has no fear behind her'.

Phoebe, a surname of Diana or Artemis (like Phoebus, title of Apollo), means 'the bright', and is applied to her in her character of the goddess of the moon: so often used simply for the Moon, or, as here, the night.

The story about the Bear varies, but Ovid (II. 153) tells it thus:

Callisto, daughter of Lycaon, an Arcadian king, was beloved by Iuppiter (Zeus) to whom she bore a son. Iuno (Here) in her jealousy changed her into a bear, and her son one day saw her and chased her. He was just about to slay her when Iuppiter interposed, and changed the She-bear into the Bear Constellation, and her son into the Bear-warden or Arctophylax (also called Bootes, the brightest star of which is Arcturus). Ovid here makes his lines still more obscure by calling the son *Lycaon*, the name of his grandfather.

The Bear never sets, being too near the pole (in these latitudes): So Ovid means, in plain English: 'On 7 June Arctophylax sets (at sunrise), and the Bear's Watcher is thus removed'. (The *true* morning setting is 28 May, the apparent 10 June: so this is fairly accurate. See Introduction, *Astronomy*).

237. The Fishers' Festival (Ludi Piscatorii), held on 7 June in fields near the Tiber (in whose honour they were, 238); and the day was a holiday among the men of that craft. [*Campus* usually means the Campus Martius: but Festus tells us the feast was held on the other (W.) side of the river.]

240. *cibis,* 'bait'.

[241—248. 8 June: Festival of the Temple of Mens and its history.]

241. After the disastrous battle (in 217 B.C.) of Lake Trasimene, in the second Punic War, where the consul Flaminius and his army perished (*leto consulis,* 243), the Romans vowed several temples; among these, the praetor Otacilius vowed one to 'Mind', Mens, which was built two years later on the Capitol (Liv. XXII. 10). Ovid says that this piety succeeded, and their affairs were managed better afterwards (246).

242. The Romans always called the Carthaginians 'faithless . There is no evidence that Hannibal ever broke his word, while the Senate on more than one occasion were shamelessly treacherous. Yet Livy (XXI. 4), speaking of Hannibal, attributes to him 'perfidia plus-quam Punica'.

243. *rebellaras,* lit. 'renewed the war', but it has the association of *revolting* connected with it, and suggests that the second Punic War was a rising of the *conquered*.

244. *Mauras,* strictly 'Moor' (Morocco and Algiers): but used loosely of Africans.

246. *illa,* Mens. Cf. note on 241.

247. 'Sees the Ides approach with six days intervening', an elaborate way of saying, 'is six days before Ides', i.e., a.d. VI. Id. Iun. or 8 June.

[242—468. 9 June: Festival of Vesta.

The goddess comes to the poet (249—256). Origin of the Temple, and why it was round (257—282). The priestesses, the symbol, the name, the offerings assigned to Vesta (283—310). The Vesta-day, the holiday of bakers; and asses also assist in the festivities (311—348). Account of the altar to Iuppiter Pistor on the Capitol: story of the Gauls besieging the Capitol, and how they threw out loaves to them, and thus the siege was raised (349—394). Reason why on the Vestalia the matrons walk barefoot to the temple (395—416). Story of the Palladium (417—460).

Anniversary of Brutus' victory in Spain and Crassus defeat in Asia (461—468).]

Page 28.

249. *operata. Operor* is used in a special sense of 'performing religious rites', 'paying homage'. Here it is used of the poet's homage: 'to thee we open our duteous mouth', or 'in thy service we open', taking *tibi* with *operata*, which is rather better.

There does not seem to be anything past about *operata;* it is the poetic use of these past participles instead of the pres., like 'longum cantu splata laborem percurrit pectine telas (Verg. *G.* I. 293).

250. *venire*, metaphorically 'to treat of'.

251. *totus eram*, a vivid idiom 'was deep in': comp. *multus esse, nullus esse.*

253. *valeant*, 'farewell'. This profession of avoiding the poetic trick of divine visions is only a trick the more.

256. i. e. the goddess inspired him with the knowledge though there was no vision.

257. *Parilia* was the shepherds' festival on the 21st April, when the flocks and herds were purified with burning of sulphur and herbs and laurel boughs, sprinkling water, &c., in honour of the shepherds' god *Pales* [PA-'feed', cf. *pasco, pastor,* &c.]. It was kept as the foundation-festival of Rome, as Romulus was related to have founded the city on that day. (*Palilia* orig. prob. corrupted to *Parilia*, as *medidies* to *meridies*.)

So, 'had had 40 Parilia'=had been founded 40 years; and so the inauguration of Vesta is put in the second year of Numa (Romulus reigning 38 years), acc. to the mythical chronology.

259. *placidi,* 'peaceful'.

260. *numinis,* gen. after *metuentius,* acc. to the common use when a part. is used as adj. (*alieni appetens, servantissimus aequi,* &c.).

Livy says of Numa (1. 18), 'deeply versed in human and divine law'.

Sabina. Numa was a native of Cures in the Sabine country, 20 m. N.E. of Rome.

261. *videres,* strictly used, 'you would have seen'.

The primitive shrine was a wicker-work hut thatched.

263. *Vesta's* round temple was just in front of the Palatine, and the Regia in front of that.

264. *intonsi.* Pliny says that shaving was introduced at Rome 300 B.C. Scipio Africanus (VI. 234) is said to have been the first Roman daily shaved. Hence the old Romans are often called *intonsi.*

266. *causa probanda subest,* 'there is a reason that can be made good', 'there is a cause to shew'.

268. The MSS. here read: *significant sedem terra focusque suam,* which may be construed, 'the earth and the fire mark their dwelling', i.e. Vesta, identified with earth, marks her dwelling (by the shape, which resembles that of the earth): and the fire, which belongs to both, by being ever present in the temple.

But this is very intricate, and obscurely expressed, if that is the meaning; and I have adopted Peter's ingenious reading, *significantque deam tecta focusque suam',* 'the building (by its shape) and the fire are the signs of their goddess': a sense which keeps the same general connection, and is much simpler and clearer.

271—278. A curious passage, which some people have rejected, as it has been considered irrelevant, and 271—276 is wanting in many MSS.

The omission from the MSS. however is easily explained, as 270 and 276 both end with *onus,* and the copyist, having written 270, might easily carry on his eye by mistake to 277: a common source of error. Moreover the sense is really quite intelligible and defensible.

The theory, dating from Anaxagoras, seems to have been that the earth was a sphere in the centre of the universe, which itself revolved, while the earth was stationary. Outside the earth were the spheres of the other planets, revolving each round the same centre.

271. 'Its very roundness keeps the orb poised, and there is no projection to overbalance any part': they conceived the tendency *to fall* counteracted by its symmetrical shape, there being nothing to make it heavier on one side than another. See 275.

272. *premat*, subj. of purpose, final.

274. *latus*, 'side' of the universe.

275. *convexa*, 'spherical': if the shape had been irregular, there would have been more weight in one direction: and thus the *centrality* (and so the *balance*) would have been spoiled.

277. Archimedes, the great mathematician of Syracuse (287—212 B.C.), constructed a globe representing the universe, with the heavenly bodies made to move inside: something like what we call an orrery.

Page 29.

279. Being a sphere and in the centre, it is symmetrically placed with reference to the outside sphere.

282. *tholus* (a Greek word), the round dome at the top of Vesta's temple.

283. *virginibus ministris*, 'with maidens to attend her'. See 44, where the construction is explained.

285. *Ops*, the Italian goddess of Produce or Fertility, imagined as the wife of *Saturnus* [SA-'sow'], the god originally of seed or sowing. When the Greek mythology was known to the Romans, an identification took place of the various divinities, and the Greek legends became inextricably interwoven with the old Roman rustic notions. Thus Saturn was identified with Κρόνος, whose daughters were Here (Iuno), Demeter (Ceres) and Hestia (Vesta): and even their mother Rhea was identified with Ops. Often the names alone remain to shew the original difference of deities, the more imaginative Greek stories about them being fully adopted.

288. *viri*, gen. after adj. 259.

293. *remittit nec capit*, i.e. is neither fertilized nor fertile, neither receives seed nor gives produce: *semina* in two slightly different (though both natural) senses.

294. *comites virginitatis*, 'comrades of her maidenhood', i.e. maidens like herself'.

295. This refers to Book III. 45, where Ovid said, 'Vestae simulacra feruntur virgineas oculis opposuisse manus', as though there were a statue: an odd mistake, which he now corrects.

O. F.   5

299. *vi stando Vesta*, a very fanciful and of course impossible derivation. The poets generally (and Ovid particularly) are fond of such fancies: and in days before etymology the origin of words was not felt to be a question of fact, but a fair subject for ingenuity and imagination. (So Plato gives ἔρως from ἐρρωμένος, ἵμερος from ἰόντα μέρη, &c.). Compare 301, 303. See 140.

300. i. e. Ἑστία from ἑστάναι, 'to stand'.

301. Ovid is more fortunate with this etymology: for probably fo-cus and fo-veo are connected [FA- or FAV- 'bright', so 'warm'].

302. *tamen* here is almost = 'by the way': it is opposed to something understood '(though now in the interior of the house), yet then', &c.

303. *vestibulum*, another fancy derivation. The real origin is probably VAS- 'to dwell'.

304. *praefamur* 'first address': orig. a Greek custom, to begin with Vesta.

305. Sense:—The older custom was to eat the family meal before the common hearth, and so in the presence of the gods: thus the old Sabine goddess of Leisure (Vacuna) was worshipped, the worshippers sitting as well as standing: and the custom of giving Vesta her plateful is a relic of the old rites.

scamnis longis, 'on long benches', because in the poet's day they dined on couches, three on a couch, round the table in the centre (triclinium).

310. *pura patella*, 'a plain dish', not such as you might fancy the gods would have. The point is the simplicity, which is a sign of its antiquity.

Page 30.

311. Now he describes the bakers' festival on the Vestalia or 9 June. It was a holiday of the household, and so of all those who made bread: including the donkey which turned the flour-mill.

panis dependet, for they hung the bread round their necks. See 347.

312. The *mola* or mill in its old form was a cone of stone standing up on a firm base with a hollow cone fitting over it. This top stone had a funnel shaped hole in the top down which the corn was put: the upper stone was then turned and the corn ground between the surfaces. It was made of various hard stones, sometimes a kind of lava (*pumiceas*, 318). It was, of course, rough (*scabra*) to do its work.

313. *sola farra* (not bread, but), 'simple spelt': the earliest food of the rustic Romans being parched spelt. Madvig, however, ingeniously suggests *tota* or *solda* (*solida*): since *sola* is unlikely.

314. *Fornacalis dea*, 'the goddess of baking' or 'of the ovens', a rustic worship of the regular Roman practical type.

316. potsherds (*tegula quassa*) were placed on the hot ground under the fire, and the bread baked on them under the ashes.

The connexion of the sense is a little obscure, but it is as follows ;— The Vestalia is the bakers' feast. In old days there was no bread, only parched spelt : that had nothing to do with Vesta, the *hearth* goddess, for an oven was used for parching : the goddess there was 'fornacalis dea' who has also her rites. But the earliest *bakers* used the *hearth* for the purpose, and so are connected with Vesta.

318. *pumiceas*, 312.

319—346. Story of Priapus.

319. *Praeteream* called *deliberative* subj. 'must I pass over?'

Priapus a rustic god, the promoter of fertility both in plants and animals. The centre of his worship was Lampsacus on the Hellespont (345). The Romans revered him as the god of the country produce, and the protector of the woods and fields and farms, and his statue was a rude wooden image painted red (333).

320. *ioci*, gen. of quality, 'a merry little tale'.

321. *Cybele* the Phrygian 'mother of the gods', a deity imported from Asia, with a set of Phrygian myths attached to her name. She was supposed to have invented the art of fortifying cities, and wore in embattled crown (*turrigera* &c.) as a symbol. So *turrita* Verg. *Ae.* vi. 786.

323. The *Satyrs* were strange beings connected with the worship of Dionysos (Bacchus) the god of wine. They were half-human in shape with little horns and goats' tails, and pointed ears. They were merry beings, given to sensual pleasures, dancing, and rude jests. The head of the troop was called Silenus (326), who is an old Satyr, a kind of nurse and instructor to the youthful Bacchus, and who is usually drawn as a jovial red-faced ugly old man, riding on a donkey, and fond of drink.

324. *quamvis* in poetry is often used with indic.

327. *temere* 'at random', 'at pleasure'.

332. *fulta caput* 'her head resting', see 92.

333. *ruber*, see 319.

335. *putarit*, indirect quest., 2.

340. *lene*, acc. of adj. used often as adv. in poetry, 'chiefly with verbs of bodily action' (Roby 1096), as *acerba tuens, dulce ridentem, magnum loqui*, &c.

Page **31.**

346. *apta,* 'a fit offering' to Priapus.

347. *diva,* Vesta, for it was her festival.

de pane monilibus, the prep. *de* depending on subst. *monilibus,* a poet. construction. In prose it would have a partic. or adj. (*factis,* or *longis,* &c.) to depend on. Compare *oculos sine lumine,* II. 845, *sine labe iuventam,* IV. 235, &c.

For sense, see 311.

349. *arce,* 'in the citadel', poet. use of the local abl. without prep.

Tonantis, 'the Thunderer': the Temple of Iuppiter Tonans was built by Augustus on the Capitol proper (see 18) in gratitude for his preservation from a flash of lightning, which killed a slave of his in Spain when carrying a torch before his litter. It was inaugurated 1 Sept. 22 B.C.

350. *Pistor,* lit. the 'pounder', so 'the baker'. The story is given here.

351. *Gallis.* The abl. (as often with soldiers) without prep., as they are regarded as instruments. The allusion is to the famous siege of Rome by the Gauls, 390 B.C.

355. *Scilicet,* [*scire licet* 'you may know'] 'doubtless', here as often ironical.

356. *dolor animi* opp. to *voce querentis.*

360. *impositurus,* 'to set over', i. e. 'to make mistress of'.

361. *suburbanos.* The Aequi, Latins, and Hernici had all been practically incorporated before the Gauls came; the Volscians soon after.

Etruscaque: before 390, Rome had made very little way north; but Ov. is clearly thinking of the capture of Veii six years before, which was a great step in advance.

362. *in cursu,* 'advancing'.

lare, 95. Often used for 'house', 'home'.

363. When the Gauls entered Rome, the older patricians (according to the splendid tradition) who could not be of use in defending the Capitol, sat each in the vestibule of his house, in his white toga with purple border, the badge of office; those who had won triumphs in the *toga picta* or embroidered toga ('*picta veste*'), and sitting on the ivory chair of office: and thus seated were all murdered by the Gauls.

Ovid speaks of them all as if 'triumphales', by an allowable poetic exaggeration.

aerata, 'brazen', i.e. 'adorned with brass': he is speaking of the primitive times.   Others read *reserata* 'open', *cerata*, &c.

365.   *pignora* were the mysterious relics kept in the inmost sanctuary of Vesta, which were regarded as the 'pledge' or guarantee of Rome's stability.   Cf. Liv. XXVI. 27 : 'Vestae aedem et aeternos ignes et conditum in penetrali *fatale pignus* imperii Romani'.

What they were exactly, no one knew : it was one of the priestly secrets : but the Palladium was one of them, see 437 sqq.

Iliacae, 227.

transferri, because on the approach of the Gauls the fire and relics and Vestal virgins were taken for safety to Caere (20 m. N.W. of Rome) in Etruria.

366.   'Doubtless they fancy there are some gods', 'they still believe in them it seems !' ironical, of course.

367.   *respicerent*, impf. because *they do not regard it*.   See 10 and Scheme.

in arce, instead of saying '*arcem in qua*' the subst. passes into the rel. sentence : a common attraction.

370.   *perire*, 'are lost', 'are vain'.

372.   *si non poterunt*, i.e. 'if you will not allow them'.

Page 32.

373.   *victus*, common gen. after adj. and verbs of *lacking* or *plenty*.

375.   Quirinus (Romulus) as the first augur of Rome had the augur's badge, a crooked staff (*lituus*) and a toga with purple horizontal stripes (*trabea*).

377.   *publica*, i.e. 'to all of us gods'.

istis, 215.

379.   *Effice putentur*, 'See they be supposed'.   The subj. is really the *jussive*, dependent on another verb.   The more regular prose construction after *efficio* would be subj. with *ut*, which would then be classed as *consecutive*.   Both forms are usually called Oblique Petition.

381.   *cava machina*, 312.

388.   *opem*, 'resource', 'treasure'; 'strength'.

389.   *ambages* [ambi = ἀμφί old prep. 'around', and *ag*-], lit. 'driving round', so 'a roundabout way' and by metaphor 'a dark saying', 'a riddle', 'a hard question'.

390.   *quam*, interrog.

391.   *Ceres*, goddess of the earth, and esp. of corn, identified (285)

with Greek Demeter [δᾶ-μήτηρ, mother Earth], and often put simply for 'corn'.

395—416. [Origin of the custom of the Matrons walking barefoot to the temple of Vesta. MSS. read *illa qua:* i. e. *illa* (adv., orig. *via* understood) 'that way', 'in that direction'. But Madvig's emendation *illa quae* is a much better reading: the construction is so much simpler.]

396. The *Via Nova* went from the Velabrum, a lower district near the river, past the N.W. side of Palatine, round its N. corner, (so approaching close to the forum, 396) and along its N.E. face. See Map.

399. *vicina loci*, rare use of gen. after *vicinus*, perhaps a Greek imitation: 'when near the spot she saw me'.

401. This story points to a tradition which is one among many indications that in old days the Tiber water was much higher than in recent times, and much of the ground about, that in historic times was dry, was once lake or swamp. Thus the valley between the Palatine and Aventine (Circus Maximus 405), the valley between the Palatine and Capitol (Velabrum 405), the *lacus Curtius* in the forum, (403), the marsh in the Campus Martius (Palus Caprea), are all probably old swamps fed by Tiber water. The myths of Vertumnus who turned back the flood (410), and Romulus and Remus being floated ashore on the Palatine slope, are other signs of the same thing. (Burn, p. 21, 599.)

402. *fossa*, 'a hollow', *here* natural, properly artificial.

redundatis, special poetic use of the passive, though the verb is properly intrans. 'to overflow'.

Page 33.

403. There are two stories given by Livy for the origin of *lacus Curtius:* (1) I. 12: in the old days the Sabines from the Capitol and the Romans from the Palatine met in the valley between to fight: the Sabine leader Metius Curtius, being defeated, plunged his horse into the swamp and so escaped. This was on the site of the forum Romanum. (2) VII. 6: a huge cavity opened in the forum B.C. 362, and the augurs said that if Rome was to be saved, 'that for which she was preeminent' must be buried in the chasm. M. Curtius, a Roman warrior, interpreted this to mean 'Valour and arms', and adorning his horse splendidly, jumped in full armour into the gulf, which closed over him.

405. *pompa* [πομπή, Greek word, from πέμπω 'send' or 'escort'] 'procession', with which the Circus games always began: it was half

a religious ceremony, the gods' statues being carried. As they started from the forum, they would go through Velabra into the Circus.

Velabra, plur. for there were the greater S.E., and the less, N.E.

406. *cassa*, 'empty', so 'useless'.

407, 408. i.e. 'you crossed in boats'.

409, 410. The allusion is to the god Vertumnus. The name is clearly Latin, and means the 'god of change' [-mnus is related to Greek -μενος of partic. and appears in autumnus, alumnus, damnum, columna, &c.], originally of the changes of the season, the flowers to fruit, &c. Symbolically, the god himself was said to change into all shapes, which explains 409. The name also gave rise to the absurd story of his having *turned* back the Tiber *flood* (verto-amnis), based on a false derivation.

[417—460. Story of the Palladium, or image of Pallas (Minerva).]

419. Ilus, great-grandson of Dardanus (42), built Ilion or Troy.

420. *Asia*, here seems to mean Phrygia or the Troad merely.

421. The statue of Pallas was said to have been hurled by Iuppiter down upon Troy, and Ilus built a shrine to it. When Troy was sacked, the Palladium was taken away, and many cities (Rome among the number) claimed to have the original Palladium : each city naturally inventing a different story to account for it, (433).

423. Ovid had travelled in Greece, Asia, and Sicily as many young Romans did. These two lines are parenthetic.

424. Two MSS. read *illi;* a worse sense.

425. *Smintheus*, a surname of Apollo (*Il.* I. 39), said to be from σμίνθος, a field-mouse, perhaps because he cured the plague of field-mice for the people of the Troad. He is 'consulted' as the god of prophecy.

426. *mentito*, 'lying', 249.

427. *aetheream*, because of the way she came to them, 421.

430. The order of kings of Troy from father to son was Ilus, Laomedon, Priam : in the latter's reign came the capture.

432. *iudicio*, of Paris, 16.

Page 34.

433. *genus Adrasti*, Diomedes, son of Deipyle, daughter of Adrastus, succeeded his grandfather as king of Argos. He was a chieftain in the Trojan war, and did great exploits. Acc. to Vergil, he and Ulixes (Ulysses) stole the Palladium (*Aen.* II. 164). Another story attributed this to Aeneas.

434. *datur,* 'is given', poet. variation for 'is recorded'. [The MSS. read mostly *ferunt,* which Madvig defends !]

435. i.e. 'whoever brought it, it is ours'.

tuetur, 'protects us'.

437. The temple of Vesta caught fire in the year 241 B.C., and the story how Metellus saved the Palladium and sacra is here told.

439. *sceleratis ignibus,* abl. inst. 'the sacred fire (i.e. the temple) was burnt with fire unholy'. The next line expresses the same idea more simply.

440. *flammae.* The dat. is used with *misceo* instead of the more common abl. (or abl. with *cum*) occasionally in good authors.

445. *pignora,* 365.

fatalia, 'fateful', for the destinies of Rome were supposed to hang on them, 365.

449. he 'drew water as a purification for the impiety of profaning 'the spot where no man might enter.'

450. *vir,* opp. *femina.*

viro, the reg. dat. after gerundive, the orig. meaning being 'places not for a man to enter'.

451. 'On my head let vengeance for the deed o'erflow': for such a violation of a holy place even for a good end might bring wrath on Rome. It is curious to reflect what a low idea of the gods this implies: that they might be so stupid as to punish the courageous devotion which rescued their 'sacra'. In this case however Vesta was belied.

454. *Pontificis,* for Metellus was *pontifex maximus,* who as chief of the sacred college at Rome had charge of all the religious ceremonies, and special right therefore to interfere to save the *sacra.*

455. Augustus made it one of his chief cares, after the establishment of his power at Rome, to restore the temples and religious ceremonies: and among the chief of these was the old Vesta-worship.

457. Vestal virgins were bound to the oath of chastity. If any broke the vow, she was held 'to have defiled her fillet' (a woollen band worn round her head as a sign of her office) and was buried alive. Notice that he says 'buried in the living earth', instead of 'buried alive in the earth'. This is a very startling instance of the *transferred epithet,* which in milder forms is common: thus we say 'a flying shot', 'a feverish night', 'a faithful promise'. So Verg. *Aen.* XII. 859 says of an arrow ' *celeres* incognita transilit umbras'.

459. i.e. 'the punishment is appropriate to the offence'.

[461—468. Anniversary of Brutus' victory in Spain and Crassus defeat in Asia.]

461. The Gallaeci (Ovid uses the Greek form Callaici), were the inhabitants of the N.W. corner of Spain, now Galicia, and were subdued 136 B.C. by D. Iunius Brutus, in a great battle, where 50,000 of them are said to have fallen (Momms. III. 19 E.T.). The date of the battle was 9 June. Brutus received the surname Gallaecus from this exploit. (Strictly his *cognomen* was Brutus, and this was his *agnomen*.)

Page 35.

465. On the same day of the month, B.C. 53, M. Licinius Crassus was defeated by the Parthians near Carrhae in Mesopotamia: he and his son were killed, and the army was utterly routed with great slaughter, and the standards of the legions were taken by the Parthians. This reverse rankled in the minds of the Romans: and they were proportionately rejoiced, when Augustus by a mixture of diplomacy and threats induced the Parthians, in B.C. 20, to send back the standards.

468. *vindicet,* after *qui,* subj. of purpose (final).

[469—472. 10 June. Rising of the Dolphin.]

469, 70. When the feast is over (469) and the mills set to work again (470). (*Ceres,* 391.)

471. The Dolphin, a small constellation of four bright stars, whose sunset-rising was about 10 June. Ovid, however, below (720) gives another date, 17 June; see Introduction, § 6.

[473—562. 11 June: Matralia and Feast of Mater Matuta (473—484). Story of Ino (485—550). Customs of the feast (551—562).]

473. Sense: 'morning breaks'.

Tithonus was the beautiful son of Laomedon (430), the king of Troy, (hence called *Phrygian*): *Aurora* (the dawn) stole him for love, and he became her husband. Every day she rose early for the daybreak, and left him lonely.

474. *Lucifer,* properly the 'morning star' or the planet Venus, well known in Homer's time, though it was thought distinct from the evening star. It is often mentioned as the accompaniment of dawn: often as the dawn itself (211).

475. The festival of *Mater Matuta,* an old Italian goddess of the morning (cf. *matutinus*), was especially observed by the matrons: as she was regarded as a goddess who had power over children.

But later there grew up an identification (such as we have noticed above, 285) of Matuta with Ino; and thus the Greek story of Ino became entangled with the Roman idea of Matuta.

Ino, sister of Semele (who was beloved by Zeus, and became by him mother of Bacchus), brought up the young child, and thus incurred the anger of the jealous Here. The goddess drove *Athamas* (husband of Ino, 489) mad, and he killed his son *Learchus* (490), fancying him a lion (489). Ino and *Melicertes* (or Melicerta, 494), the other son, fled, (Athamas also imagined them to be lions), and leaped in despair from a rock on the isthmus of Corinth (495) into the sea. *Panope* and the other sea-nymphs (499) received them, and they become sea-powers under the new names of *Leucothea* and *Palaemon* (501).

This was the Greek story which Ovid adopts, but he makes the end of it Roman again, thus:—The new sea-gods are led to the Tiber-mouth; they find (near the site of Rome) the Arcadian Evander settled; and the women excited to bacchic fury by Iuno attack the new comers, who are only rescued by Hercules. Ino is received by the mother of Evander, the prophetic Carmentis, who recognises her; and she and her son are installed as Sea-gods of Rome under the Roman names of Matuta and Portunus.

The temple of Mater Matuta was near the river, not far from Forum Boarium: see Plan.

The 11th of June was the festival of the Matralia, when the Matrons went into this temple, with their sisters' children, not their own: no slaves were admitted (481), except one, who was dismissed with a slap in the face. The real origin of these singular customs was no doubt Latin and primitive, being a symbol of the feeling that children should be the care of all matrons, and not of careless slaves.

476. *Thebanae*, for Ino was daughter of the Theban king and founder Cadmus.

liba, 'baked cake', the matron's offering.

477—8. The *area* was the old *forum boarium* or 'cattle market' near the river, close to the two bridges (*pontibus*) *Aemilianus* and *Sublicius* on one side, and the *circus Maximus* on the other, see 401.

480. *Servi*, S. Tullius, who was reputed the founder of the temple.

483. *racemiferos*, for Bacchus was pictured as crowned with ivy and vine.

484. *domus*, 'household'. See story, 475.

485. Semele had begged Iuppiter to appear to her in the same majesty as he had when with Iuno. He warned her of the danger, but

she persisted, and when he came in power with the thunder around him she was consumed. The infant Bacchus was rescued, but Semele 'was burnt up with Jove's compliance', as Ovid says.

487. *intumesco*, naturally, of anger and jealousy; at such care being taken of the 'son of a concubine'.

488. *Educet*, this subjunctive is common in sentences which give a reason *as felt* or *as alleged:* the clause being then practically oblique. Thus 'Socrates accusatus est quod *corrumperet* iuventutem', Socrates was accused [not 'because he corrupted', which would be indic. but] '*of corrupting* youth', the ground being that *alleged by the accusers*.

sanguis, i long. This is perhaps a return to the *old* quantity, for the *is* of sanguis was originally long, and is always so used in Lucretius (cf. IV. 1049), and once in Vergil, *Aen.* X. 487.

ille, Bacchus, was Ino's sister's son : see 475.

489. *imagine falsa*, 'delusion'. He thought they were lions, see 475. *hinc*, from Iuno's wrath.

Page 36.

491. *umbras*, 'the shades', i.e. the spirit. The body was burnt, and perfume, oil, dainties, &c., sometimes garments, thrown on the fire (*omnia iusta*). See *Aen.* VI. 225.

496. *terra* is the nom. and he means the isthmus of Corinth, which is 'hemmed in a narrow space' and 'beats back two seas'—the Saronic and Corinthian gulfs. So Corinth is called by Horace and Ovid '*bimaris*'.

499. *Panope* one of the 100 (otherwise 50) Nereids or sea-nymphs.

501. *nondum* qualifies only the names: 'She, not yet (called), Leucothea, the boy, not yet (called) Palaemon, reach the mouths, &c.'

502. *verticibus*, 'eddies'.

503. *Stimula*, i. e. 'the goddess of Frenzy' (*stimulo*, 'to goad') apparently identified with Semele, mother of Bacchus, as suited both the thing and the name.

504. *maenadas Ausonias*, 'the Latin bacchanals'. *maenas* a Greek word μαινάς, lit. 'raving', used of women frenzied by the inspiration of Bacchus. The declension (-*as* short) is Greek. The *Ausonii* were an old Italian tribe in the W. of Campania, and the name is one of the numerous poetic synonyms for 'Italian'.

505. *foret*, past, because *quaerit* is historic present, so equivalent to a past.

Arcadas (Greek form). The old tradition was that an Arcadian king, Evander, with his people was found by Aeneas (when he landed in Italy) settled on the site of the future Rome. Vergil uses this tradition in the *Aeneid* (VIII. 51, &c.).

507. *Saturnia*, Iuno, daughter of Saturn.

dissimulata deam, a remarkable example of the construction explained 92: *deam* is used where strictly we should have the abstract word 'her divinity', by a stretch of construction. Construe: 'hiding her godhead'.

508. *fictis*, 'false'. The rapidity of the narrative is remarkable. The appearance on the scene of Iuno is all left to the imagination.

509. *faciles*, i,e. 'easily beguiled', 'simple'.

pectore, i.e. 'sense.

captae, 204.

512. 'She has with her a pledge (i.e. her son Melicerta) wherewith (i.e. by loss of which) she can be punished'.

quo is grammatically instr. abl. *possit:* for subj. see 3.

514. *Thyiades* (tri-syll. Greek word) from stem θυ- 'rave', common Greek name for the 'frenzied Bacchanals'.

515. *pugnant*, 'struggle', by a (not unnatural) stretch of construction with inf., as after words of desire.

516. *ignorat adhuc*, as a new comer.

518. *Aventini*, the hill of Rome just S. of the Forum Boarium.

519. Hercules (called *Oetaeus*, because Herakles, the Greek hero with whom he was identified, was burnt to death on mount Oeta in N. Greece) drove, acc. to the story, the oxen of the monster Geryon from Spain, and stopped on his way at Rome, near a cave on the Aventine. Here lived the giant Cacus, and the tale of his fight with Hercules is told splendidly in Verg. *Aen.* VIII. 193. Also cf. *Fasti*, I. 543: and 80 supra.

Hiberus, means 'Spanish', being the Greek name.

Page 37.

524. *numen*, Iuno, who from jealousy (as H. was the son of Iuppiter and Alcmena) persecuted him from his birth upwards.

525. *partim*, orig. acc. of *pars*, but used adverbially: sometimes even w. nom. as 'partim eorum fuerunt, qui', &c.: here for acc.

526. *continet*, 'checks': apparently she kept back the suicide, 498.

527.   *ut est velox*, 'swift as it is'.   *Comparative* ut; not 'as it is swift', *causal*, which *ut* never is.   So 493.

528.   *in ore*, i.e. of the people.

529.   *Carmentis*, an Italian goddess (or nymph) of prophecy (car-men), the chief of the Camenae (song-goddesses), afterwards identified with the Greek Muses.   She was regarded as the mother of Evander, and had a temple near the Capitol, and one of the gates just under the Capitol was called after her *porta Carmentalis*.

531.   *Tegeaea*, 'Arcadian', from Tegea, a town of Arcadia in S. Greece.

532.   *subito*, i.e. 'hastily lit'.

534.   *arte*, 'than skill': it was a simple, but kindly welcome.

537.   *caelum...sumit*, a picturesque and vivid phrase for inspiration.

544.   *vestris*, i.e. 'your new' domain.

545.   See 475.
Grais (Greek name) 'Greeks': for dat. see 108.

546.   *in*, 'over'.

547.   *Portunus*, old Latin god of 'harbours': later identified as here.

548.   *aequus*, 'propitious', lit. 'fair'.

550.   Notice the rapidity, observable all through this tale, and especially at the end.

551.   See 475.

Page 38.

553.   Athamas, husband of Ino (*Cadmei*, see 76), secretly loved one of Ino's handmaidens, and from her learnt that roasted seeds were given to the farmers.

558.   *odio sit*, called the *predicative* dat., 'is for hatred', 'is for you to hate', i.e. 'is hateful'.   The use is thus confined to words of an *abstract* character.

The dative is really of the same class as 'decemviri legibus scri-bundis', 'commissioners *for drawing up* laws'.

559.   Reason why the matrons bring *not their own* children.   See 475.
adoret, 'would supplicate', i.e. 'would naturally, or rightly, not, &c.'

560.   As Learchus was killed by Athamas, and Melicerta Ino threw into the sea.

[563—568.   On the same day fell Rutilius, 90 B.C., and Didius, 89, in Social war].

563. In 90 B.C. the Social war, as it is called, broke out. Many of the Italian tribes (or 'allies' of Rome), the Marsi, Peligni, Samnites, &c., revolted because the Senate refused to listen to their grievances. The consul P. Rutilius Lupus was defeated and killed on the Liris (according to the common account), the main river of S. Latium. Ovid places the scene on the Tolenus (565), a river which rises in the Marsian hills not far from the Liris, but flows N. to the Nar and Tiber.

564. *luce mea,* 11 June.

ab, because *cades* = 'thou shalt be slain'.

565. *exitus,* 'fulfilment'.

567. *Pallantide.* Ovid makes Aurora ('the dawn') daughter of Pallas ; and thus *Pallantis* is an artificial and fanciful word for 'morning'.

568. T. Didius had been consul nine years before. We infer from this line that he was fighting as an officer in this war, and fell 89 B.C.

opes, 'power'.

[569—636. Commemoration-day of the Temple of Fortune: three accounts of the image.]

569. There was in the Forum Boarium also a temple to Fortuna (not to be confused with that of Fors Fortuna, below, 773), ascribed to Servius Tullius. There was here a mysterious image, covered with two togas, of which Ovid gives three conjectural accounts.

lux, 11 June: *auctor,* Servius Tullius: *locus,* forum Boarium.

572. *mentis,* gen. of reference, common in Augustan poets after adjectives, in imitation of Greek.

[573—580. One suggestion is, that the goddess who secretly loved Servius, now keeps his image in her temple, but veiled, from modesty.]

573. *dea.* The goddess Fortune (usually blind, 576) was said to have loved and secretly wedded the king Servius.

578. *porta Fenestella,* wrongly supposed to have been a gate of Rome; probably an arch within the walls so called, to which Ovid gives this origin. (Burn, p. 51.)

Page 39.

[581—584. Second suggestion: the grief of the people at the death of the peaceful king was inconsolable as long as they *saw* his statue: so they veiled it.]

583. *imagine,* 'from his image', abl. inst. or cause.

[585—636. Third suggestion: when the wicked Tullia, after her father had been murdered, entered the temple, the image hid its face, and asked for a covering to be thrown over it: this was done.]

585. *spatio*, 'course': and the metaphor is continued in the next line, the sense being, 'I will treat the long story briefly'.

586. *adductos*, 'reined in'.

intus, 'on the inner edge', and so a shorter course.

587. The famous legend of the death of Servius. His daughter Tullia, wife of the good Aruns Tarquinius, had conspired with Lucius Tarquinius, husband of her gentle sister. They had murdered each their own spouse, and married each other. Lucius ejected Servius from the throne, and sent assassins to slay him. Tullia rode triumphantly to the forum to salute Lucius king; and finding her father's body in the way, bade the charioteer drive over it.

590. *pia*, 'good': i.e. 'if we do not slay my father': for *pius* is especially used of good behaviour to *parents* and *kindred*, see 90.

593. *facio dotale*, 'I make my dowry'.

595. *Regia res scelus est.* The infamous sentiment thus tersely expressed by the wicked Tullia suited well with the traditional Roman hatred of the *name* of king: though Rome had had the *thing* ever since Julius Caesar made himself master of the city.

600. *socero*, dat. after *rapta*, verb. of 'taking away'.

601. *Esquiliis* (see Map), the straggling hill N.E. of Palatine, the nearer portion being called the Oppius, where the palace of Servius lay. The top of the street up from the curia or senate-house in the forum to the palace was the 'vicus sceleratus'.

604. *ferox* [stem DHAR- 'firm', 'strong', whence *firmus, fortis*, &c.], 'bold', 'proud'.

606. *corripit*, prop. 'seizes': then by obvious metaphor 'chides'.

607. i.e., 'if you don't go, you will get a bitter reward, &c.' A natural form to put the threat into.

608. *invitas*, it is more picturesque to *transfer the epithet* from the driver to the wheels, as though the chariot itself refused the impious deed: see 457.

610. *nota*, 'infamy'.

Page 40.

613. *sub imagine*, 'in the form of'.

620. *positi pudoris*, 'of shame abandoned', i.e. 'of unchastity'.

623. *Romano amictu*, the toga, 570.

626. *Mulciber*, old Latin title of the fire-god (Volcanus), afterwards identified with Hephaistos; according to the old tradition Vulcan was the father of Servius, and Ovid connects this with the tale that a tongue of fire was seen on Servius' head when a babe. Livy, however, says: 'patre nullo', i.e. his father was unknown, and the common notion was that his birth was humble; see 782.

628. *Corniculana*, a captive from Corniculum, old Latin town not far from Rome.

[637—648. 11th of June was also Commemoration-day of the Temple of Concord in the porticus Livia. Augustus' example of simplicity of life.]

637. *Te dedicat*, for in Latin they could say either 'to hallow the temple' or 'to hallow the god', i.e. the image.

638. *quam*, 'Harmony, which Livia assured to her lord', i.e. Livia as the loving wife was the right person to dedicate the temple of Harmony.

641. *urbis opus*, i.e. 'as huge as a city'.

643. *nullo sub crimine regni*, 'from no charge of regal ambition', like Valerius Poplicola, who being charged with a desire to become king, because he was building a fine house on the top of the Velia (slope above lower end of forum), came before the people with lowered fasces (he was consul) and promised to remove it. This is the charming tale told by Livy (II. 7). Augustus' virtue, the poet means, was higher still, as he did the popular act of his own impulse.

647. *censura*, Augustus added (B.C. 29) the censorship to his other powers: the chief object of which was, under cover of the old constitutional forms, to give him complete control of the roll of the Senate.

648. *vindex*, 'defender, maintainer, of the right'.

Page 41.

[649—710. The 12th has no distinguishing mark: on the Ides, 13th, is the commem. of a temple of Iuppiter Invictus (649—650); and the Quinquatrus minores. Origin of flute-players' procession, and why they wore the matron's *stola* (651—692): origin of the name: flutes the invention of Minerva (693—710).]

649. *possis*, for subj. see 3.

651. *Quinquatrus* was the name of a festival to Minerva on 19 March, prop. called so from being *five* days after Ides. [Ovid (III. 809) gives a different reason, viz. that they *lasted* five days, but we know that

orig. they were only for one day.] Ovid says *this* feast was called
Q. *minores,* as being also Minerva's feast, since she invented the flute
(696).

On this day (13 June) flute-players went in procession masked,
and clad in the stola or matron's dress, through the city to Minerva's
temple.

654. *per-sona* [son- 'sound through'], an actor's mask, which
covered the head. *Stola* [Greek στολή 'dress'], a long dress reaching
to the feet; the regular costume of the Roman matrons.

655. *Tritonia,* old title of Pallas (identified with Minerva). Origin
unknown. Homer calls her Τριτογένεια.

659. *fanis,* &c. ablatives of *occasion.*

662. *quod frangeret,* 'such as destroyed', consec. See 3.
Graia ars, 'the Greek art' is of course the 'flute-playing'.

Livy (IX. 30) gives the story of this persecution of the Flute-players
as follows :

The flute-players, being forbidden by Appius Claudius and Plautius
the censors to feast in the temple of Iuppiter (an old right of theirs),
seceded to Tibur. The Senate sent to ask the Tiburtines to manage that
they should return. The Tiburtines accordingly asked them to a feast,
made them drunk, and sent them back to Rome in waggons, where
they awoke next morning in the forum. It was agreed that they should
remain, the right be restored to them, and the annual festival and
license of roaming through the city be given to them.

663. i.e. Further the aedile had restricted to ten the fluteplayers at
funerals.

irent, because it is dependent on the oratio obliqua.

665. *exilio mutant urbem,* 'exchange the city for exile' we say:
but *exilio* is abl.

666. i.e. what a little way they had to go for exile! See 61, and
Introduction, p. 7.

667. *quaeritur,* 'is missed'.

668. *supremos toros,* a natural expression for the bier, especially
when we remember that the richer classes always carried their dead to
the pyre on couches (*lecticae*), sometimes very splendid ones of ivory
adorned with gold and purple.

nenia, here used for the flute-playing, was strictly the funeral-song
in praise of the dead sung by the *praeficae* or hired women-mourners.

674. *praecomposito,* 'prepared beforehand', i.e. with a face of dra-
matic surprise and horror.

676. i. e. 'your *patronus* is coming'.

When a man wished to free (*manu mittere*) a slave, he brought him
to the magistrate and stated his wish. The lictor laid a rod upon the
slave's head, pronounced a form of words, and he was free. He then
became a *libertus* or freedman, and his late master was his *patronus*.
The patronus still had considerable claims for service upon the freedman; which explains the (pretended) fright of the messenger when he
is said to be coming.

vindicta is the name of the rod used in this ceremony: and here by
a natural extension stands for the 'manumission'.

Page 42.

679. *dominus*, 'the master' of the house.

plaustro, abl. of place, common in poetry 'lifted *on* the waggon'. In
prose this would be 'in plaustrum'. Or more simply, it may be merely
the instrumental abl. 'lifted with the waggon': i.e. the waggon carried
them.

680. The *plaustrum* is only the truck, or bottom board with wheels:
the body of the waggon is here wicker (*scirpea*).

685. *Plautius*, 662. *specie numeroque*, his wish was to conceal them
by a double disguise, dressing them as women, and increasing their
number.

686. *tegi*, in prose would be *ut* with *subj.*

689. *notentur*, 'censured': the regular word for the censor's repri-
mand.

695—6. Sense : 'The Quinquatrus in March (*Martius*) is my feast :
and the flute-players' festival being mine also (since I invented the flute)
is called by the same name'.

697. *buxo*, for box-wood was commonly used for flutes.

701. *tanti*, gen. price (prob. old locative), 'worth so much', i.e. as to
spoil my beauty.

703. *Satyrus*, 323. This is the famous myth of the satyr Marsyas,
who challenged Apollo, was beaten, and punished for his audacity by
being flayed. It is a subject of many works of art.

Page 43.

705. *concipit*: the description is rather loose: for *concipio* properly
means 'to draw in, receive', as opposed to 'emitting'; and to this *digitis*
will not apply. The line is quite natural however: 'with his fingers he
now lets out the air, now takes it in'.

708.   Observe the rapidity of all this description, in this particular
line it becomes ghastly.

[711—716.   15 June: Rise of Hyades: cleansing of Vesta's temple:
to-morrow begins the S.W. wind.]

711.   *Tertia*, what we should call the second, i. e. after Ides, the 15th.

Thyene, one of the stars forming the cluster of the Hyades, see 197.
The apparent morning rising was strictly on the 9th June, so that this is
a week wrong.   See Introduction, p. 13.

Dodoni, as according to one account these nymphs of Dodona in
Epirus were changed by Zeus into the seven Hyades.

712.   The Hyades are placed in the forehead of the Bull, one of the
Zodiac signs: and Ovid here identifies this bull with the one whose form
Zeus assumed, when he carried off Europa (daughter of Phoenician king
Agenor, hence *Agenorei* 712) from the shore where she played to Crete.

713.   See 227.

716.   *secundus*, partic. form from *sequor*, lit. 'following : so often
used of a wind astern, 'favourable'.

[717—719.   16 June.   Evening rising of Orion.]

717.   *Heliades*, the daughters of Helios, Greek name for the Sun · so
this is a fanciful and elaborate line for 'sunset'.

718.   Curious use of *stella* singular for 'the stars'.

719.   *Hyriea:* Hyrieus a Boeotian hero was the father of Orion a
giant hunter, who became the well-known constellation.

As to the rising of Orion, see *On the Astronomy*, Introduction, p. 16.

[720—724.   17 June.   Evening rising of the Dolphin.   Anniversary
of the victory of Postumius Tubertus over Aequi and Volsci.

720.   *Delphin*, the Dolphin which saved Arion, when he leapt into
the sea, from gratitude for his sweet singing, was put among the stars,
and became the constellation so called, whose evening rising is dated
17 June.   See 471.   The story is beautifully told *Fasti* II. 83.

721.   The reference is to the battle B.C. 431 on Algidus, the northern
spur of the Alban hills.   Livy (IV. 26) tells the story thus : The consuls
being defeated by the enemy, were ordered by the Senate to appoint a
dictator.   They refused, and the Senate appealed to the tribunes, who
forced them to do so.   Postumius Tubertus was appointed, and he
Aequi and Volsci were defeated and their camp taken.

hic, the dolphin.

724.   *niveis*, for the triumphal car was drawn by white horses.
Ovid calls him Postume instead of Postumi, apparently for metrical
purposes.

Page 44.

[725—728. 19 June. The Sun passes from the Twins to the Crab (signs of the Zodiac) : Festival of Minerva on the Aventine.]

725. Elaborate expression for 13 days (we should say the 12th day) before 1 July; i.e. 19 June.

728. On the South side of the Aventine there was a temple of Minerva of ancient date. Its exact site is unknown.

[729—762. 20 June. Commemoration of Temple of Summanus : evening rising of the constellation of the Snake-holder ; and the story of the same being set in the heavens, viz. how Aesculapius revived Hippolytus, and was slain by Iuppiter but interceded for by Apollo.]

729. 'The daughter-in-law of Laomedon' was Aurora, see 473 : so this is another elaborate couplet for 'day breaks'.

731. *Summanus,* obscure. Latin deity, said to be the god of night-thunder : an odd function. Ovid himself does not seem to know much about him.

Pyrrhus, king of Epirus, a famous general and freebooter who waged war with Rome B.C. 280—275 and gave the Romans considerable trouble and alarm (compare 203).

733. *hanc,* 'this day'.

Galatea, a sea-nymph (beloved by Sicilian Acis, who was slain by the jealous Cyclops). The line is only an elaborate Ovidian phrase for 'the day sinking in the western sea'.

735. The allusion here is to Aesculapius, the Healer. He was son of Apollo (761) and Coronis (746), and was noted for the art of healing, being even able to raise the dead. He raised the dead Hippolytus, but was slain by Iuppiter for the arrogant act. Phoebus interfered, and he was placed among the stars as the Man holding the Snake (Ophiuchus or Serpentarius).

surgit humo, the constellation rises. See Introduction § 6.

avitis, because, being the son of Apollo, Aesculapius was the grandson of Iuppiter.

736. *nexo angue,* a variation of phrase for *nexas angue.* ' With the snake tied round them '. [The MSS. have unintelligibly *gemino nexas :* there was only one snake, probably altered to get an easier construction.]

The snake was the symbol of Aesculapius.

737. Phaedra, wife of Theseus, king of Athens, fell in love with her stepson Hippolytus. He, as a votary of the chaste Diana (745), was pure, and repelled her love. She accused him falsely to her hus-

band of having tempted her, and Theseus cursed his son and drove him
from home. As he was flying to Troezen (in Argolis) Poseidon sent
a bull (740) out of the sea, which frightened the horses : they ran away,
and threw Hippolytus out of the car; but as he was entangled in the reins
he was dragged over the rocks and killed. Aesculapius was at hand
(Epidaurus near Troezen was the centre of his worship) and healed him.

739. *impune,* 'safely.'

750—3. These three lines refer to the story of Glaucus, the son of
the Cretan king Minos, who was drowned in a honey-cask. Minos
ordered the Argive seer Polyidus to raise him to life, and being unable
he was shut up in the vault with the body. A snake glided to the
body, and Polyidus killed it. Presently came another snake and
dropped a herb on its dead companion, which revived. Polyidus then
covered Glaucus with the herb, and revived him.

751. *observatas,* 'watched' by Polyidus. [The reading here is
Merkel's conj. Most MSS. have the unintelligible *augur descendit in
herbas;* and then *anguis ab angue.*]

Page 45.

755. *Dictynna* [δίκτυον, 'a net'], a name of the huntress Diana.
When Hippolytus was restored to life, Diana hid him in the grove of
Aricia (in Latium on the Appian way) whence he was called Virbius
(according to Ovid from *Vir-bis,* 'twice a man,' from his resurrection
to life). But this was a later addition; the old Greek tale knows
nothing of his recovery, and Horace says (*Od.* IV. 7. 25), 'Diana cannot free the pure Hippolytus from the nether darkness.'

756. The *lacus* is the lovely lake of Nemi, a round volcanic basin
in the Alban hills, close behind Aricia.

757. *Clymenus,* a late Greek name for Hades or Pluto, god of the
lower world. *Clotho* [Κλωθώ, 'the spinster'], one of the Three Fates,
who spins the thread of man's life.

These two feel that raising the dead is an encroachment on their rights.

761. *placare,* 'be reconciled', 'forgive'.

[763—768. 23 June. Anniversary of Trasimene : a bad day for
military enterprise.]

763. *quamvis* in prose has subj. 324.

765. See 241, note.

766. *Volucres,* 'birds', i. e. omens. Livy tells us (XXII. 3) that
just before the start the consul's horse threw him, and the standard re-
mained immoveably fixed in the ground.

767. *temeraria tempora*, 'the rash day' (epithet transferred, 608), for the Romans marched on in defiance of the omens.

768. *quartus bis*, 'eighth' day from end, i. e. 23 June.

[769—784. 24 June: Anniversary of the defeat of Syphax, also of the Metaurus victory. Festival of Fors Fortuna, founded by Servius Tullius.]

769. At the close of the second Punic War, Scipio (the great Africanus) obtained the aid of Masinissa, Numidian prince, against Syphax, king of the western Numidians. After burning Syphax's camp, Masinissa and the Roman legatus Laelius pursued him to Cirta and took him prisoner This was in 203 B.C.

770. *Hasdrubal*, brother of Hannibal, marched (207 B.C.) into Italy to join his brother; but was met by the Romans and defeated at the famous battle of Metaurus, where his army and camp were annihilated.

Livy says (XXVII. 49) that when he found all was lost, he spurred his horse into the midst of a Roman cohort, and, as was worthy of Hamilcar's son and Hannibal's brother, died fighting.

Ovid puts the suicide in a slightly different form.

773. There were three temples of Fors Fortuna at Rome: this one, founded by Servius Tullius (according to tradition), was on the right bank of the Tiber, at the sixth milestone. The festival was 24 June, and it was, as we see, a day of merry-making among the lower classes and slaves.

776. *munera*, buildings founded by individuals were called *munera* 'bounty' or 'gift': thus *Art. Am.* I., 'Muneribus nati sua munera mater addidit', i.e. 'she added the portico of Octavia to the theatre of Marcellus'.

Page 46.

781. *de plebe*. Servius was of humble origin, acc. the old story that his mother was a slave: see note on 626.

784. *dubia*. Fortuna was naturally called 'Uncertain'.
propinqua, being *outside* Rome, 773.

[785—790 26 June. Rising of the belt of Orion; and the solstice.]

785. The connection of this with the last, by the idea of drunken reveller returning from the feast and then remembering it was two days to the rising of the belt of Orion, is unusually artificial and frigid, even for Ovid. For Astronomy, see Introduction, p. 16.

[791—794. **27** June. Festival-day of the Temple of the Lares, and of Iuppiter Stator.]

791. *Lucifero subeunte,* i.e. after Ovid's manner ' on the next day'.

Lares. The Sacred Way, approaching the forum from the S.W., mounts a slight rise. On the top stands now the arch of Titus, and this part was called Summa Sacra Via. To the left, on the Palatine side, stood the Sacellum Larum, a little further came the cross-road leading to the chief gate of the Palatine, close to which stood the old temple of Iuppiter Stator. This, according to the tradition (Liv. I. 12), was vowed by Romulus in the Sabine war, if he *stayed* the flight, and an altar (and afterwards a temple) was built upon the spot.

792. There were small shops in the Sacra Via, and we may suppose from this line that the people who sold flower chaplets had their stalls here.

[795—796. **29** June. Commem.-day of Temple of Quirinus.]

795. i.e. three days remain, or as we should say ' two': it is the inclusive method of counting, which strikes one especially when the number is small. 29 June is a. d. III. Kal. Jul., and so he says there are three days left.

Parcae are the Fates; Clotho, Lachesis, Atropos.

796. *trabea,* 375.

The old Sabine god Quirinus was identified with Romulus: and his temple was on the S.E. side of the Quirinal, towards the Viminal.

[767—812. **30** June. Festival of the Temple of Hercules and the Muses. Clio gives the poet an account of it.]

798. *Pierides,* old Greek name for the nine Muses: said to have been from a place Pieria near Mt Olympus.

The 'Aedes Herculis Musarum', as it was called, was built by Fulvius Nobilior, who defeated (Liv. XXXIX. 5) the Aetolians, B.C. 187. It was restored by L. Marcius Philippus (son of the Marcius consul 56), who married Atia, an aunt of Augustus (*matertera Caesaris,* 809). His daughter Marcia (802) was married to a friend of Ovid's. The temple lay between Circus Flaminius and the river. The genealogy is confused by the fact that Marcius Philippus the father, consul 56, married the *elder Atia,* Augustus' *mother,* when her first husband Octavius was dead.

addite summa, ' put an end '.

800. i.e. to whom Iuno at last gave way (*do manus* by obvious metaphor from a prisoner begging quarter), and allowed him a place in Heaven.

801. *Clio,* the muse of history.

Page 47.

803. *Anco,* Ancus Marcius, fourth king of Rome.

sacrifico. Livy (I. 32) tells us 'he paid the greatest attention to performing all the divine services according to Numa's institution'.

804. Observe the very rare construction of *par* with abl. *par cum* and abl. is common enough, and this is a poetical extension of that. Ovid has the same const. (almost the same line) with *impar* (IV. 306), 'Nec facies impar nobilitate fuit'.

807. *laudamus,* i.e. 'we Muses'.

812. *Alcides.* Hercules is often so called, being grandson of Alcaeus, who was the father of Amphitryon.

lyram. Fulvius had brought from Greece some terra-cotta statues of the Muses by Zeuxis, and one of Hercules playing on the lyre : this we learn from Pliny.

SCHEME OF
THE USES OF THE LATIN SUBJUNCTIVE WITH
REFERENCES TO THIS BOOK.

1. OPTATIVE and JUSSIVE, (wish or command).

(a) *direct :*
 faciat *or* utinam faciat. [219, 371, 415, 656, 701] *Optative.*
 'may he do *or* would he might do it !'
 faciat, 'let him do it'. [41, 381].
 ne feceris, 'don't do it'. [*nec* for *ne*, 807].
  and the rare past jussive used as conditional.
 dixisset, 'let him have spoken', i. e. 'suppose he spoke'. [113].

(b) *indirect :*
 effice putentur, 'cause them to be thought'. [379].

(c) *interrogative :* [Dubitative or Deliberative].

 1. *direct.* quid faciam? 'what *am* I to do?' [319].
  quid facerem? 'what *was* I to do?' [149].

 2. *indirect :*
  nescio quid faciam } 'I don't (or did not) know what
  nesciebam quid facerem} to do'. [29, 213].

2. FINAL, (Purpose).

(a) *with* ut, ne, &c. :
 doceo, ne facias, 'I teach you, that you may not do it'. [25 &c.].

(b) *with* qui :
 mitto qui faciat, 'I send a man to do'. [272, 468, here or 3, 6].

(c)   *with* dum *implying purpose :*
maneo dum faciat, 'I wait till he does it'.
or priusquam :
non abibo priusquam faciat, 'I will not go away before he does it'.

3.   CONSECUTIVE (Result).

(a)   *with* ut :
tantum est ut timeam, 'it is so great that I fear'.

(b)   *with* qui, (*so* quin &c.) :
non is sum qui faciam, 'I am not the man to do it'. [3, 512, 649, 662].

4.   CONDITIONAL.

(a)   *Principal verb,* (Apodosis) :
faciam *or* fecerim, 'I would do'. [764].
facerem *or* fecissem, 'I would have done' (*or,* 'have been doing,' *impf.*). [275, 369].
(*without* Protasis, often called POTENTIAL, [71, 89, 100, 539, 559]. *so with* forsitan.
forsitan facias, 'perhaps you may do'. [72]).

(b)   *Dependent verb* (Protasis) :
si facias *or* feceris, 'if you should do'. [764].
si faceres *or* fecisses, 'if you had done' (or 'had been doing' *impf.*) [10, 275. 367].

5.   CAUSAL.

(a)   *cum*
cum faciat, 'since he does'. [273].

(b)   *qui :*
culpo te qui facias, 'I blame you for doing it'.

(c)   *attendant circumstances :* cum (impf. and plupf.).
cum hoc faceret, 'when he was doing this.' [14, 221].

6.   CONCESSIVE.

(a)   *conjunctions.* (quamvis, dum, &c.).
quamvis faciat, 'though he does'. [232].

(b)   *qui.*

7. ORATIO OBLIQUA.

(a) *statement:* only in dependent clauses.

dixit se quod vellent facturum, 'he said he would do what they wished'. [164, 663].

So when the clause is really, though not in form, oblique, called VIRTU-
ALLY OBLIQUE.

irascor quod facias, 'I am angry, on the ground (*or* at the idea) that you do it'. [488].

(b) *question :* (indirect interrogative).

nescio quid faciat, 'I don't know what he is doing'.

[2, 12, 103, 123, 169, 222, 335, 386, 390, 481, 551, 710.]

(c) *oblique petition.*

oro facias, 'I beg you to do'.

oro ut *or* ne facias, 'I beg you to do,' or 'not to do'.

efficio ut eas, 'I cause you to go '.

These Subjunctives can however be further analysed, and have already
been given above in 1 (*b*), 2, and 3.

[This list includes all the common uses of the Lat. subjunctive.]

VOCABULARY

ABBREVIATIONS

acc.	accusative.	*interr.*	interrogative.
adj.	adjective.	*m.*	masculine.
adv.	adverb.	*n.*	neuter.
c.	common.	*num.*	numeral.
comp.	comparative.	*perf.*	perfect.
conj.	conjunction.	*pl.*	plural.
defect.	defective.	*possess.*	possessive.
dep.	deponent.	*prep.*	preposition.
f.	feminine.	*pron.*	pronoun.
impers.	impersonal.	*sup.*	supine.
indecl.	indeclinable.	*vb.*	verb.
interj.	interjection.	1, 2, 3, 4.	conjugations.

ā, ăb, prep. *by* (a person), *from*

abeo (eo), *go away*

ābicio (iacio), *cast away*

abscondo (condo), *hide*

absum (sum), *am absent, distant from*

accēdo (cedo), *approach, am added*

accĭpio (capio), *receive, hear*

accurro (curro), *hasten towards*

actum, -i, n. *deed*

ad, prep. *to, at, towards*

addo (do), *add*

addūco (duco), *bring to, rein in*

adeo (eo), *approach, visit*

adeō, adv. *so far; truly*

adhūc, adv. *still, as yet*

adiăceo (iaceo), *lie near*

adĭtus, -ūs, m. *entry, approach*

adiungo (iungo), *join to, associate*

admisceo (misceo), *mix, combine*

admitto (mitto), *admit*

adōro, 1, *worship, supplicate*

adsum (sum), *am present*

aduncus, adj. *hooked, with hooked talons*

adventus, -ūs, m. *arrival*

adўtus, -i, m. *shrine*

aedes, -is, f. *temple*, pl. *house*

aedilis, -is, m. *aedile*

aequo, 1, *make equal, level*

aequus, adj. *just, equal, favourable*

Aequus, -i, c. *Aequian*

āër, -is, m. *air*

aerātus, adj. *brazen*

aes, aeris, n. *bronze*

aetas, -ātis, f. *age, time of life*

aeternus, adj. *eternal*

aethēr, -ěris (acc. -ěra), *air, sky*

aethĕrius, adj. *of the air, soaring*

aevum, -i, n. *age, generation*

afflo, 1, *breathe on, inspire*

Ăgēnŏrĕus, adj. *of Agenor*

aggrĕdior, aggressus, dep. 3, *approach, address*

ăgĭto, 1, *excite, shake, hunt*

agnosco (nosco), *recognise*

ăgo, ēgi, actum, 3, *act, do, perform, drive; age, come*

āio, defect. vb. *say*

āla, -ae, f. *wing*

albus, adj. *white*

Algĭdus, adj. *of Algidus*

ălĭēnus, adj. *strange, unsuitable*

ălĭquis, pron. *some one, some*

ălĭter, adv. *otherwise*

ălius, adj. *other*

allĭcio, -ui, -itum, 3, *entice*

alloquor, allocūtus, dep. 3, *speak to*

ălo, -ui, -itum, 3, *feed, rear*

Alpīnus, adj. *Alpine*

alter, pron. *the one or the other*

altus, adj. *high*; n. pl. *sea*

ălumnus, -i, m. *nursling, charge*

ămārus, adj. *bitter*

ambāges, -is, f. *riddle, circuit*

ambo, -bae, adj. *both*

ămictus, -ūs, m. *robe*

ămīcus (f. -a), *friendly*

amnis, -is, m. *river*

ămo, 1, *love*

ămor, -ōris, m. *love*

amplexus, -ūs, m. *embrace*

an, conj. *or* (interrogative)

ancilla, -ae, m. *handmaiden*

anguis, -is, c. *snake*

angŭlus, -i, m. *corner, projection*

ănĭma, -ae, f. *life, soul*

ănĭmal, -is, n. *animal*

ănĭmus, -i, m. *mind, feeling, courage*

annĕ, conj. see **an**

annuo, -ui, -utum, 3, *nod to, assent*

annus, -i, m. *year*

antĕ, adv. or prep. *before, forward*

antīquus, adj. *ancient*

antrum, -i, n. *cave*

ănus, -ūs, f. *old woman*

ăpĕrio, -ui, -rtum, 4, *open, reveal*

ăpex, -icis, m. *tip, peak*

Apollĭnĕus, adj. *of Apollo*

appello, 1, *call*

appōno (pono), *set beside*

aptus, adj. *fit, skilled in*

ăqua, -ae, f. *water*

ăquĭla, -ae, f. *eagle, standard*

ăquōsus, adj. *watery*

āra, -ae, f. *altar*

arbĭtrium, -i, n. *judgment, sway*

arbor, -ŏris, f. *tree*

arbŭtĕus, adj. *of the wild-strawberry*

Arcăs, -adis, c. *Arcadian*

arceo, 2, *keep off*

ardeo, arsi, arsum, 2, *burn*

ārea, -ae, f. *open space, threshing-floor*

Ārĭcīnus, adj. *of Aricia*

arma, -orum, n. *arms*

armĭfer, adj. *bearing arms*

ăro, 1, *plough*

ars, -tis, f. *art, skill*

artĭfex, -ficis, c. *artist, musician*

artus, -ūs, m. *limb*

ărundo, -dinis, f. *reed*

arx, -cis, f. *citadel*

ascītus, adj. *foreign*

Ascraeus, adj. *of Ascra*

ăsellus (f. -a), *small ass*

ăsĭnus (f. -a), *ass*

asper, adj. *rough, harsh*

aspĭcio, -spexi, -spectum, 3, *look, behold*

assentio (sentio), *agree*

assĭduus, adj. *constant, tireless, undying*

astrum, -i, n. *star*

at, conj. *but*

atque, conj. *and*

ātrium, -i, n. *hall*

attingo (tango), *reach, touch, attain*

attŏnĭtus, adj. *amazed, terror-stricken*

auctor, -ōris, c. *author, cause, founder*

audeo, ausus, semi-dep. 2, *dare*

audio, 4, *hear*

aufĕro (fero), *bear away*

augeo, auxi, auctum, 2, *increase*

augur, -is, m. *augur*

aura, -ae, f. *breeze*

aurĕus, adj. *golden*

aurīga, -ae, m. *charioteer*

aurītus, adj. *long-eared*

aurum, -i, n. *gold*

Ausŏnius, adj. *Ausonian (Italian)*

auspĭcium, -i, n. *auspices, sanction*

auxĭlium, -i, n. *aid*

Āventīnus, adj. or noun, *Aventine*

āversus, adj. *turned back, averse*

ăvĭdus, adj. *greedy*

ăvis, -is, c. *bird*

ăvītus, adj. *of a grandfather, ancestral*

ăvus, -i, m. *grandfather*

Baccha, -ae, f. *a Bacchanal*

barbărus, adj. or noun, *barbarous, barbarian*

bellum, -i, n. *war*

bĕnĕ, adv. *well, fairly, fully*

bĭbo, bĭbi, 3, *drink*

bĭmenstris, -e, adj. *two months old*

bīni, -ae, -a, distrib. num. *two, two each*

bīs, adv. *twice*

blandior, dep. 4, *flatter, coax*

bŏnus, adj. *good, kind*

bōs, bŏvis, c. *ox*

bracchium, -i, n. *arm*

brĕvis, adj. *short, scanty, brief*

brĕvĭter, adv. *briefly*

buxus, -i, f. *box, wood*

cădo, cĕcĭdi, cāsum, 3, *fall, happen*

caecus, adj. *blind*

caedes, -is, f. *bloodshed, death*

caedo, cĕcĭdi, caesum, 3, *slay, cut*

caelestis, adj. *heavenly*

caelum, -i, n. *heaven*

caespes, -pitis, m. *turf*

călesco, 3, *grow warm*

călĭdus, adj. *warm*

campus, -i, m. *plain, Campus Martius*

Cancer, -cri, m. *crab, sign of the Zodiac*

candĭdus, adj. *white, bright*

cānĭtiēs, -ei, f. *gray hairs*

canna, -ae, f. *reed, cane*

căno, cĕcĭni, cantum, 3, *sing*

cănōrus, adj. *tuneful*

canto, 1, *sing*

căpesso, -ivi, -itum, 3, *take hold of, take up*

căpillus, -i, m. *hair*

căpio, cepi, captum, 3, *take, seize*

Căpĭtōlīnus, adj. *of the Capitol*

Căpĭtōlium, n. *Capitol*

capto, 1, *woo*

captus (capio), adj. *deprived of* (with ablative)

căput, -pitis, n. *head, chief*

carbăsus, -i, f. (pl. -a) *sails*

cardo, -dĭnis, m. *hinge*

carmen, -mĭnis, n. *song, spell, charm, oracle*

carpentum, -i, n. *carriage*

carpo, -psi, -ptum, 3, *pluck, tear, gather*

cărus, adj. *dear*

cassus, adj. *vain, hollow, empty*

castra, -orum, n. *camp*

castus, adj. *chaste*

causa, -ae, f. *cause, theme*

căveo, cāvi, cautum, 2, *beware, guard against*

căvus, adj. *hollow*

cēdo, cessi, cessum, 3, *go, retire, yield*

cĕlĕber, adj. *frequented, renowned*

cĕlĕbro, 1, *frequent, honour, celebrate*

cĕler, cĕleris, cĕlere, adj. *swift*

cēlo, 1, *hide*

celsus, adj. *lofty*

censūra, -ae, f. *censorship*

centum, indecl. adj. *hundred*

Cĕriālis, adj. *of Ceres*

certāmen, -minis, n. *contest*

certus, adj. *certain, fixed, aware*

cesso, 1, *cease, be slow to*

cētēri, -ae, -a, adj. *rest, other*

chŏrus, -i, m. *dance, throng*

cĭbus, -i, m. *food, bait*

cingo, cinxi, cinctum, 3, *surround, enclose*

cĭnis, -ĕris, m. *ashes*

circus, -i, m. *circus, games*

cĭtŏ, adv. *quickly*

clāmor, -ōris, m. *shout, uproar*

clārus, adj. *famous, bright*

classis, -is, f. *fleet, class*

claudo, clausi, clausum, 3, *shut*

coctus (coquo), adj. *cooked*

cŏeo (eo), *come together, combine*

coepi, coeptum, 3, *begin*

coeptum, -i, n. *enterprise, undertaking*

coeptus (coepi), adj. *begun*

cŏerceo, 2, *check, control*

cŏētus, -ūs, m. *crowd, throng*

cognōmen, -minis, n. *surname*

cognosco, -nōvi, -nĭtum, 3, *know, ascertain*

collēga, -ae, m. *colleague*

collum, -i, n. *neck*

cŏlo, -ui, cultum, 3, *worship, cultivate*

cŏlōnus, -i, m. *tiller*

cŏlor, -ōris, m. *colour, complexion*

cŏlumna, -ae, f. *column*

cŏma, -ae, f. *hair, leaves*

cŏmĕs, -itis, c. *companion*

commendo, 1, *entrust, recommend*

commissum, -i, n. *crime*

commūnis, adj. *common, general*

compĕrio, -peri, -pertum, 4, *discover*

complector, -plexus, dep. 3, *embrace*

compleo, 2, *fulfil, fill up*

concha, -ae, f. *shell*

concĭdo (cado), *fall down*

concĭpio (capio), *conceive, entertain, take in*

concĭtus, adj. *excited, roused*

Concordia, -ae, f. *Concord*

concumbo, -cŭbui, -cŭbĭtum, 3, *lie with*

condĭtor, -ōris, m. *founder, chronicler*

condo, -didi, -ditum, 3, *found, relate, hide*

confĕro (fero), *compare, bestow, bring together*

confūsus (confundo), adj. *disturbed, perplexed*

coniŭgium, -i, n. *wedlock*

coniunx, -iugis, c. *husband or wife*

consīdo, -sedi, -sessum, 3, *settle, sit down*

consĭlium, -i, n. *plan, advice, wisdom*

constat, impers. *it is agreed*

constĭtuo, -ui, -ūtum, 3, *set up, determine*

consŭl, -is, m. *consul*

consŭlo, -ui, -sultum, 3, *consult, advise*

contĭceo, 2, *be silent*

contingo (tango), *reach, attain, happen*

contĭnuō, adv. *straightway*

contĭnuus, adj. *next, following*

contrā, adv. and prep. *against*

contrăho (traho), *draw in, attract, confine*

contundo (tundo), *bruise, crush*

convĕnit, impers. *it is fitting, suitable*

convexus, adj. *spherical*

convīva, -ae, c. *guest*

convīvium, -i, n. *revel-band*

convŏco, 1, *call together*

convŏlo, 1, *fly*

cor, cordis, n. *heart*

Cornĭcŭlānus, adj. *of Corniculum*

cornū, -ūs, n. *horn*

cŏrōna, -ae, f. *crown*

cŏrōno, 1, *crown, wreathe*

corpus, -oris, n. *body*

corrĭpio (rapio), *carry away, overpower, chide*

Corsus, adj. *Corsican*

cŏruscus, adj. *flashing*

crās, adv. *to-morrow*

crēdo, crēdĭdi, crēdĭtum, 3, *believe, entrust*

crēdŭlus, adj. *trustful, believing*

crĕmo, 1, *burn*

creo, 1, *create*

cresco, crēvi, crētum, 3, *grow, thrive*

crimen, -mĭnis, n. *charge, crime*

crīnis, -is, m. *hair*

crūdus, adj. *raw*

cruor, -ōris, n. *blood*

cultus, -ūs, m. *worship, garb*

cum, conj. *when, since, though*

cum, prep. *with*

cumba, -ae, f. *skiff*

cūnae, -arum, f. *cradle*

cŭpīdo, -dĭnis, f. *desire, greed*

cŭpio, -ivi, -itum, 3, *desire*

cūr, adv. *why?*

cūra, -ae, f. *care, thought, attention*

cūro, 1, *attend to, care for*

currus, -ūs, m. *chariot*

cursus, -ūs, m. *course, onrush*

curvus, adj. *curved*

cuspis, -pidis, f. *spear*

custos, -ōdis, c. *guardian, protector*

cŭtis, -is, f. *skin*

damno, 1, *condemn*

damnum, -i, n. *loss, harm*

dăpes, dapis, f. *banquet*

dē, prep. *from, down from, concerning, according to*

dĕa, -ae, f. *goddess*

dēbeo, 2, *am bound to, owe*

dĕcem, indecl. adj. *ten*

dĕcet, impers. *it becomes, is fitting*

dēcurro (curro), *run down*

dĕcus, -ŏris, n. *honour, glory*

dēdĕcus, -ŏris, n. *dishonour*

dēdĭco, 1, *dedicate*

dēdūco (duco), *derive, bring from*

dēfendo, -di, -sum, 3, *defend, uphold*

dēfensor, -ōris, c. *champion*

dēfero (fero), *bestow, submit, carry down*

dēfŏdio, -fōdi, -fossum, 3, *bury*

dēfungor, -functus, dep. 3, *perform to the end*

dēhinc, adv. *henceforward*

delphin, -īnis, m. *dolphin*

dēlūbrum, -i, n. *shrine*

dēmitto (mitto), *lay down, let down*

dēmo, dempsi, demptum, 3, *take away, withdraw*

dēni, -ae, -a, distrib. num. *ten each, ten*

densus, adj. *thick, close*

dēpecto, no perf., -pexum, 3, *comb*

dēpendeo, 2, *hang from, depend on*

dēpōno (pono), *lay down, lay aside*

dēprōmo, -prompsi, -promptum, 3, *broach, bring forth*

descendo, -di, -sum, 3, *descend*

dēsĕro, -ui, -rtum, 3, *desert*

dēsĭlio (salio), *leap down*

dēsĭno, -sīvi, -sĭtum, 3, *cease*

destĭtuo, -ui, -ūtum, 3, *abandon*

dēsum (sum), *am lacking*

dētonsus (dētondeo), adj. *shorn, peeled*

dĕus, -i, m. *god*

dēvŏveo, -vōvi, -vōtum, 2, *devote, dedicate to death*

dĭālis, adj. *belonging to Jupiter*

dīco, 1, *consecrate*

dīco, dixi, dictum, 3, *say, call*

dictum, -i, n. *word, saying*

dĭēs, -ēi, m. or f. *day*

dīgĕro (gero), *divide*

dĭgĭtus, -i, m. *finger*

dignus, adj. *worthy*

dīlĭgo, -lexi, -lectum, 3, *esteem, love*

dīmitto (mitto), *dismiss, lay aside, let out*

dīrĭgo (rego), *guide, direct*

dīrĭmo, -ēmi, -emptum, 3, *end, decide*

discēdo (cedo), *depart*

disco, dĭdĭci, no sup., 3, *learn*

discrĕpo, -ui, no sup., 1, *disagree, differ*

dissĭmŭlo, 1, *cloke, conceal*

distrĭbuo, -ui, -ūtum, 3, *assign*

dĭū, adv. *for a long time*

dĭūturnus, adj. *lasting*

dīversus, adj. *different*

dīvĕs, -ītis, adj. *rich*

dīvĭdo, -vīsi, -vīsum, 3, *divide*

dīvus (f. -a), *deity*

do, dĕdi, dătum, 1, *give, declare, utter, place*

dŏceo, -ui, doctum, 2, *teach*

doctus (doceo), adj. *learned*

Dōdōnĭs, f. adj. *of Dodona*

dŏleo, -ui, no sup., 2, *grieve, resent*

dŏlor, -ōris, m. *grief, resentment*

dŏmĭna, -ae, f. *mistress*

dŏmĭnus, -i, m. *master*

dŏmus, -ūs, f. *house*

dōnec, conj. *until, while*

dōno, 1, *present*

dōnum, -i, n. *gift*

dōs, dōtis, f. *dowry*

dōtālĕ, -is, n. *dowry*

dŭbĭto, 1, *doubt, hesitate*

dŭbius, adj. *doubtful, fickle*

dūco, duxi, ductum, 3, *lead, draw, build, reckon*

dŭellum, -i, n. *war*

dulcis, adj. *sweet*

dŭŏ, -ae, -o, adj. *two*

dŭplex, -ĭcis, adj. *two-fold*

dūro, 1, *make hard*

dūrus, adj. *unkind, hard*

dux, dŭcis, m. *leader*

ē, ex, prep. *from, out of, according to*

ēbrius, adj. *drunken*

ĕburnus, adj. *of ivory*

ecce, interj. *behold!*

ēdo, ēdĭdi, ēdĭtum, 3, *give forth, publish*

ĕdo, ēdi, ēsum, 3, *eat*

ēdūco (duco), *draw out, bring up*

efficĭo (facio), *effect, bring about*

effĭgĭēs, -ēi, f. *likeness, portrait*

effŭgĭo, -fūgi, -fūgitum, 3, *escape*

effūsus (effundo), adj. *immoderate, profuse*

ĕgĕo, 2, *lack*

ĕgŏ, pron. *I*

ēn, interj. *behold!*

ĕnim, conj. *for, indeed*

ĕo, īvi, ĭtum, 4, *go*

ēōus, adj. *eastern*

ĕpŭlae, -arum, f. *feast*

ĕquĭdem, adv. *at all events, truly*

ĕquus, -i, m. *horse*

ērĭpĭo (rapio), *snatch away*

erro, 1, *wander, make a mistake*

error, -ōris, m. *wandering, mistake*

ĕt, conj. *and*

Ētruscus, adj. *Etruscan*

Eubŏïcus, adj. *of Euboea*

ēvŏco, 1, *call forth*

excĭdo (cado), *fade, fall out*

excĭpĭo (capio), *receive, succeed*

exemplum, -i, n. *example, punishment*

exeo (eo), *come forth, depart*

exĭgo (ago), *demand*

exĭguus, adj. *small, scanty*

exĭlĭum, -i, n. *exile, place of exile*

exĭtus, -ūs, m. *issue, fulfilment*

expecto, 1, *await, expect*

expello (pello), *drive out*

exsorbeo, -ui, 2, *suck*

exsŭpĕro, 1, *surpass, outdo*

extĭmŭlo, 1, *goad, arouse*

extrēmus, adj. *last, farthest*

extum, -i, n. *entrails*

exulto, 1, *gloat*

făba, -ae, f. *bean*

făbŭla, -ae, f. *tale*

făcĭēs, -ēi, f. *face, appearance*

făcĭlis, adj. *easy, compliant, kind*

făcĭo, feci, factum, 3, *do, make, suppose, ensure*

factum, -i, n. *deed, reality*

fallo, fĕfelli, falsum, 3, *deceive, elude, escape*

falsus (fallo), adj. *false*

fāma, -ae, f. *fame, story, rumour*

fămes, -is, f. *hunger, famine*

fămŭlus (f. -a), *servant*

fānum, -i, n. *temple*

fār, farris, n. *coarse meal, spelt*

fās, indecl. noun (est), *it is lawful*

fastus, adj. f. dies, *a day on which business might be carried on*; fasti, *calendar*

fātālis, adj. *fated*

făteor, fassus, dep. 2, *confess*

fātum, -i, n. *fate*

făveo, fāvi, fautum, 2, *favour*

fēlix, adj. *fortunate*

fēmĭna, -ae, f. *woman*

fēmĭnĕus, adj. *female, womanly*

fĕnestra, -ae, f. *window*

fĕra, -ae, f. *wild beast*

fĕrĭo, ferii, 4, *strike*

fĕro, tŭli, lātum, 3, *bear, endure, allow, win*; f. pedem, *make one's way*; fertur, *is said*

fĕrox, adj. *proud, high-spirited*

ferrum, -i, n. *iron, weapon*

festum, n. *feast*

festus, adj. *festal*

fībra, -ae, f. *entrails*

fĭdēlĭter, adv. *faithfully*

fĭdēs, -ēi, f. *faith, trust, promise, fulfilment, proof*

fĭdius, adj. epithet of Jupiter, *god of truth*

fĭdus, adj. *trusty, faithful*

fĭgūra, -ae, f. *shape, appearance, type*

fĭgūro, 1, *represent, picture*

fīlia, -ae, f. *daughter*

fīlum, -i, n. *thread*

fingo, finxi, fictum, 3, *fashion, feign*

fīnio, 4, *end*

fīnis, -is, m. or f. *end, aim*

fīo, factus sum, *am made, become*

flăgro, 1, *blaze*

flamma, -ae, f. *flame*

flammeus, adj. *fiery, flame-coloured*

flāvus, adj. *yellow, golden-haired*

fleo, flēvi, flētum, 2, *weep*

flōrĭdus, adj. *flowery*

flūmen, -ĭnis, n. *river*

flŭo, -xi, -xum, 3, *flow*

fŏcus, -i, m. *hearth*

fŏrāmen, -inis, n. *hole, opening*

fŏrēs, -um, f. *doors*

forma, -ae, f. *form, shape, beauty*

Fors, fortis, f. *Chance* (epithet of Fortuna)

forsĭtan, adv. *perhaps*

forte, adv. *by chance*

fortis, adj. *brave*

fortūna, -ae, f. *fortune*

fŏrum, -i, n. *forum*

fossa, -ae, f. *ditch, hollow*

fŏveo, fōvi, fōtum, 2, *cherish, support*

frango, frēgi, fractum, 3, *break, crush*

frāter, -tris, m. *brother*

fraudo, 1, *harm*

fraus, -dis, f. *harm, wrong*

frēnum, -i (pl. -a), *bridle*

frēquens, adj. *frequent, repeated, crowded, populous*

frētum, -i, n. *strait, sea*

frons, -dis, f. *leaf, foliage*

frons, -tis, f. *brow, front*

frūges, -um, f. *crops*

frustrā, adv. *in vain*

frŭtex, -ĭcis, m. *shrub, under-growth*

fŭgio, fūgi, no sup. 3, *flee, escape*

fŭgo, 1, *banish, put to flight*

fulcīmen, -inis, n. *prop, pillar*

fulcio, fulsi, fultum, 4, *prop, support*

fulmen, -ĭnis, n. *thunderbolt*

fūnestus, adj. *deadly, grievous*

fūnus, -ĕris, n. *death, funeral*

fŭriae, -arum, f. *madness, the Furies*

furnus, -i, m. *oven*

furtim, adv. *by stealth*

furtīvus, adj. *stolen, secret*

furtum, -i, n. *theft, trick*

gălea, -ae, f. *helmet*

Gallia, -ae, f. *Gaul*

Gallicus, adj. *Gallic*

Gallus, -i, m. *a Gaul*

gaudeo, gāvīsus, semi-dep. 2, *rejoice*

gĕmĭnus, adj. *two-fold, twin*

gĕna, -ae, f. *cheek*

gĕner, -i, m. *son-in-law*

gĕnĭtor, -ōris, m. *father*

gens, -tis, f. *birth, tribe, family*

gĕnū, -ūs, n. *knee*

gĕnŭs, -ĕris, n. *birth, race, kind*

gĕro, gessi, gestum, 3, *wage, carry on, wear, perform*

glŏbus, -i, m. *globe, mass*

glōrior, dep. 1, *boast*

grădus, -ūs, m. *step, pace, stair*

Grāius, adj. *Greek*

grāmen, -inis, n. *grass, pasture, herb*

grandis, adj. *big*

grātus, adj. *pleasing, welcome*

grăvis, adj. *harmful, important, deep*

gusto, 1, *taste, eat of*

guttur, -ŭris, n. *throat, gullet*

hăbeo, -ui, -itum, 2, *have, hold, keep, count*

hăbĭto, 1, *dwell, inhabit*

hāmus, -i, m. *hook*

hasta, -ae, f. *spear*

haurio, hausi, haustum, 4, *draw up, drain*

hĕdĕra, -ae, f. *ivy*

hērēs, -ēdis, c. *heir*

heu, interj. *alas!*

Hībērus, adj. *Spanish*

hīc, adv. *here, hereupon*

hīc, haec, hōc, pron. *this*

hiems, -mis, f. *winter, storm*

hinc, adv. *hence, henceforth*

Hispānia, -ae, f. *Spain*

hŏnor, -ōris, m. *honour, office*

horrendus (horreo) adj. *fearful*

horreo, -ui, no sup., 2, *bristle, shiver, shudder at*

hortus, -i, m. *garden*

hospĕs, -ĭtis, m. *guest, stranger*

hospĭta, -ae, f. *guest, stranger (female)*

hospĭtium, -i, n. *hospitality, entertainment*

hostīlis, adj. *hostile*

hostis, -is, c. *enemy*

hŭmĭlis, adj. *lowly*

hŭmus, -i, f. *ground*

Hyrïeus, adj. *of Hyrieus*

ibĭ, adv. *here, hereupon*

Ĭdaeus, adj. *of Ida*

idcirco, adv. *for this reason*

ĭdem, eadem, ĭdem, pron. *same*

īdūs, -uum, f. *the Ides*

ĭgĭtur, conj. *therefore*

ignāvus, adj. *slothful, cowardly*

ignēus, adj. *fiery*

ignis, -is, m. *fire*

ignōro, 1, *be ignorant*

ignosco (nosco), *pardon*

ignōtus, adj. *unknown*

Ĭliăcus, adj. *of Ilium, Trojan*

illaesus, adj. *unharmed*

illĕ, illă, illŭd, pron. *that*

illīc, adv. *there*

illūc, adv. *thither*

ĭmāgo, -inis, f. *image, likeness, phantom, view*

imber, -bris, m. *rain, shower*

immensus, adj. *immense, vast*

impătiens, adj. *unable to endure, impatient*

impĕrium, -i, n. *sway, command, empire*

impĕro, 1, *command*

impĕtus, -ūs, m. *attack, impulse, inspiration*

impōno (pono), *place upon* or *over*

imprŏbus, adj. *wicked*

impūnĕ, adv. *with impunity, safely*

īmus, adj. *lowest*; ima, *bottom*

ĭn, prep. with acc. *in, upon* (motion towards); with abl. *in, upon* (rest)

incēdo (cedo), *advance, walk, approach*

incertus, adj. *doubtful, hesitating*

incestus, adj. *unchaste, impure*

incĭpio (capio), *begin*

inclūsus, adj. *shut up*

incŏla, -ae, c. *inhabitant*

incŏlo, -ui, -cultum, 3, *inhabit*

incrĕpo, -ui, -ĭtum, 1, *rebuke, twang*

incūria, -ae, f. *carelessness*

indĕ, adv. *thence, thereafter*

index, -dĭcis, c. *tell-tale*

indignor, dep. 1, *resent, be indignant*

ineo (eo), *enter, visit*

inextinctus, adj. *unextinguished*

infans, -ntis, adj. and noun, *infant, infantile*

infēlix, adj. *unfortunate*

infestus, adj. *troublesome, dangerous*

infirmus, adj. *weak*

inflo, 1, *blow upon*

ingĕmĭno, 1, *double*

ingĕnium, -i, n. *mind, intellect, temper*

ĭnĭcio (iacio), *lay upon, cast upon, instil*

īnĭūria, -ae, f. *wrong, injustice*

inops, adj. *helpless, poor*

inquam, defect. vb. *say*

insānus, adj. *mad, frenzied*

insĭdĭōsus, adj. *treacherous*

inspĭcio, -spexi, -spectum, 3, *gaze upon*

instĭmŭlo, 1, *goad, arouse*

instinctus, adj. *fired, aroused*

insto (sto), *impend, be at hand*

insum (sum), *be in*

intellĕgo, -lexi, -lectum, 3, *understand*

intempestīvus, adj. *inopportune*

inter, prep. *between, among*

interdum, adv. *sometimes*

intonsus, adj. *unshorn*

intro, 1, *enter*

intŭmesco, intumui, 3, *swell with pride* or *anger*

intŭs, adv. *in, inwards*

invĕnio, -vēni, -ventum, 4, *discover*

inventrix, -īcis, f. *discoverer*

invictus, adj. *unconquered*

invĭdeo (video), *envy, resent*

invĭdĭōsus, adj. *resented*

invītus, adj. *unwilling*

ipse, -a, -um, pron. *self*

īra, -ae, f. *anger*

irrumpo, -rupi, -ruptum, 3, *break into*

ĭs, ea, ĭd, pron. *this; he, she, it*

iste, ista, istud, pron. *that*

ĭtă, adv. *thus*

ĭtĕr, itĭnĕris, n. *way, road, journey*

ĭtĕro, 1, *repeat*

iăceo, -ui, -ĭtum, 2, *lie*

iăcio, ieci, iactum, 3, *throw, toss*

iăcŭlum, -i, n. *javelin*

iam, adv. *now, already*

Iānālis, adj. *of Janus*

iŏcōsus, adj. *merry*

iŏcus, -i, m. *jest, merriment*

iŭbeo, iussi, iussum, 2, *order*

iūdex, -ĭcis, c. *judge*

iūdĭcium, -i, n. *judgement*

iŭgum, -i, n. *hill, yoke*

Iūlĕus, adj. *of July*

iuncus, -i, m. *rush*

iungo, iunxi, iunctum, 3, *join*

Iūnius (mensis), adj. *June*

Iūnōnālis, adj. *of Juno*

Iūnōnĭcŏla, adj. *worshipping Juno*

Iūnōnius, adj. *of Juno*

iūs, iūris, n. *right, law, authority*

iussum, -i, n. *command*

iustus, adj. *just, right, due*

iŭvĕnis, -is, c. *young man or woman*

iŭvo, iūvi, iūtum, 1, *help, please*

Kălendae, -arum, f. *the Kalends*

lābo, 1, *totter, sink*

lābor, lapsus, dep. 3, *glide, slip*

lăbor, -ōris, m. *toil, hardship*

lăcer, -a, -um, adj. *mangled, torn*

lăcĕro, 1, *mangle, tear*

lăcertus, -i, m. *arm*

lăcrĭma, -ae, f. *tear*

lactens, adj. *tender*

lăcus, -ūs, m. *lake*

laedo, laesi, laesum, 3, *harm*

laetus, adj. *glad*

lănio, 1, *lacerate*

lapsus, -ūs, m. *fall, gliding*

lār, -is, m. *household deity; home*

lardum, -i, n. *bacon*

lătĕbra, -ae, f. *hiding-place*

lăteo, -ui, 2, *lie hid, lurk*

lătus, -ĕris, n. *side*

lātus, adj. *broad, wide*

laudo, 1, *praise, approve*

laurus, -i, f. *laurel*

laus, laudis, f. *praise, glory*

lēgo, lēgi, lectum, 3, *read, choose, pick*

lēnis, adj. *soft, gentle*

lentus, adj. *tough, pliant*

lētum, -i, n. *death*

lĕvis, adj. *light, slight*

lĕvo, 1, *rest, lift, relieve*

lex, lēgis, f. *law*

lĭber, -bri, m. *book*

līber, -a, -um, adj. *free*

lĭbet, impers. *it is one's fancy*

lĭbo, 1, *sacrifice, make libation*

lĭbro, 1, *poise, balance*

lībum, -i, n. *cake*

lĭcet, impers. *it is permitted*

līmen, -ĭnis, n. *threshold*

lingua, -ae, f. *tongue, speech*

linquo, līqui, 3, *leave, quit*

linter, -tris, f. *boat*

līnum, -i, n. *line*

lĭquĭdus, adj. *liquid, clear*

līs, lītis, f. *strife, suit*

lītus, -ŏris, n. *shore*

lĭtuus, -i, m. *augur's staff*

lŏco, 1, *place*

lŏcŭlus, -i, m. *coffer, casket*

lŏcus, -i, m. *place, room, scope*

longus, adj. *long, dreary*

lŏquor, locūtus, dep. 3, *say*

lōrum, -i, n. *thong, rein*

lūbrĭcus, adj. *slippery, gliding*

lūceo, luxi, 2, *shine*

Lūcifer, -i, m. *Morning Star*

luctor, dep. 1, *wrestle, strive*

luctus, -ūs, m. *mourning*

lūcus, -i, m. *grove*

lūdo, lūsi, lūsum, 3, *play, mock*

lūdus, -i, m. *play, jest*

lūmen, -ĭnis, n. *light, eye*

lux, lūcis, f. *light, day*

luxŭria, -ae, f. *luxury*

luxŭrĭōsus, adj. *luxurious, pampered*

lȳra, -ae, f. *lyre*

māchĭna, -ae, f. *mill*

macto, 1, *slay, sacrifice*

mădens, adj. *wet*

mădeo, -ui, 2,

mădesco, madui, 3, *grow wet*

Maenăs, -ădis, f. *bacchanal*

maestus, adj. *sad*

măgis, adv. *more, rather*

magnĭfĭcus, adj. *lordly, magnificent*

magnus, adj. *great, large, grand*

māior, comp. of above, *greater, older*

Māius (mensis), adj. *May*

mălĕ, adv. *poorly, ill-, scarcely*

mālo, mālui, 3, *prefer*

mălus, adj. *bad, poor*

mando, 1, *entrust*

māne, n. or adv. *morning, in the morning*

măneo, mansi, mansum, 2, *remain, await*

mānēs, -ium, m. *spirits of the dead*

mănus, -ūs, f. *hand, band*

mărĕ, -is, n. *sea*

mărītus, -i, m. *husband*

Marsus, adj. m. *Marsian*

Martius, adj. *of Mars*

māter, -tris, f. *mother*

mātertĕra, -ae, f. *mother's sister*

mātrōna, -ae, f. *matron, wife*

Maurus, adj. *Moorish*

mĕdeor, dep. 2, *heal, treat*

mĕdĭcāmĕn, -ĭnis, n. *drug*

mĕdius, adj. *middle, intervening*

mĕlior, comp. adj. *better, kinder*

mĕlius, adv. *better*

membrum, -i, n. *limb*

mĕmĭni, defect. vb. *remember*

mĕmor, adj. *mindful, heedful*

mĕmŏro, 1, *relate, bring to mind*

mendācium, -i, n. *lie, falsehood*

mens, mentis, f. *mind, understanding*

mensa, -ae, f. *table, feast, course*

mensis, -is, m. *month*

mentītus (mentior), adj. *lying*

mereēs, -ēdis, f. *wages, reward*

mĕreor, meritus, dep. 2, *deserve*

mĕrum, -i, n. *unmixed wine*

metuens, adj. *observant*

mĕtus, -ūs, m. *fear*

mĕus, possess. adj. *my, mine*

minĭmē, adv. *very little, not at all*

mĭnister (f. -tra), *attendant, acolyte*

mĭnium, -i, n. *vermilion*

mĭnor, dep. 1, *threaten*

mĭnor, comp. adj. *less, younger*

mĭnus, adv. *less*

mīror, dep. 1, *wonder*

misceo, -ui, mistum, 2, *mingle, confuse*

mĭser, -a, -um, adj. *unhappy, wretched*

mitto, mīsi, missum, 3, *send, let slip, utter, dismiss*

mŏdŏ, adv. *only, just now*; modo ...modo, *at one time, at another*

mŏdus, -i, m. *limit, manner, strain*

moenia, -ium, n. *walls*

mŏla, -ae, f. *meal; mill, mill-stone*

mōles, -is, f. *mass, bulk, trouble*

mollio, 4, *soften, assuage*

mollis, adj. *soft, gentle*

mŏneo, 2, *advise, warn*

mŏnīle, -is, n. *necklace*

mŏnĭmentum, -i, n. *memorial*

mons, montis, m. *hill, mountain*

monstro, 1, *point out*

monstrum, -i, n. *portent, monster*

mŏra, -ae, f. *delay, hindrance, obstacle*

mŏror, dep. 1, *delay, hang back, care for*

mors, mortis, f. *death*

mortālis, adj. *mortal*

mōs, mōris, m. *custom*

mōtus, -ūs, m. *motion*

mŏveo, mōvi, mōtum, 2, *move, stir, utter, disturb*

mox, adv. *soon*

multum, adv. *much, deeply*

multus, adj. *much, numerous, deep*

mundus, -i, m. *world, universe*

mūnus, -ĕris, n. *honour, office, tribute, duty, gift*

mūrus, -i, m. *wall*

mūto, 1, *change, exchange*

naenia, -ae, f. *dirge, spell*

nam, namque, conj. *for*

nanciscor, nactus, dep. 3, *get, find, gain*

narro, 1, *tell, relate*

nascor, nātus, dep. 3, *am born, arise*

nāta, -ae, f. *daughter*

nātāle, -is, n. *birthday*

nāto, 1, *float, am dazed*

nātus, -i, m. *son*

nauta, **nāvĭta**, -ae, m. *sailor*

nē, conj. *lest, that...not, not* (in prohibitions)

-nĕ, interrog. particle, denotes question

nec (**neque**), conj. *neither, nor*

nĕco, 1, *kill*

necto, nexui or nexi, nectum, 3, *bind, fasten*

nĕfandus, adj. *impious*

nĕgo, 1, *deny*

nēmo, -ĭnis, m. or f. *nobody, not one*

nĕmŏrālis, adj. *of the grove*

nĕmus, -ŏris, n. *grove, wood*

nĕpōs, -ōtis, m. *grandson*

nēquĭquam, adv. *in vain*

nescio, 4, *am ignorant*

nex, nĕcis, f. *death, murder*

nī, conj. *unless, if...not*

nĭhĭl or **nīl**, indecl. n. *nothing*

nĭmĭs, **nĭmĭum**, adv. *too, too much*

nĭmius, adj. *excessive, overbearing*

nĭsī, conj. see nī

nĭteo, 2, *shine*

nĭtidus, adj. *bright, sleek*

nītor, nīsus or nixus, dep. 3, *strive, press forward, lean*

nĭvĕus, adj. *snowy, snow-white*

nōbĭlĭtas, -ātis, f. *nobility, high birth, fame*

nŏceo, -ui, -ĭtum, 2, *harm*

nōdōsus, adj. *knotty, knotted*

nōlo, -ui, 3, *am unwilling*

nōmen, -ĭnis, n. *name, fame*

nōn, adv. *not*

nōnae, -arum, f. *the Nones*

nondum, adv. *not yet*

nonnĕ, interrogative particle expecting affirmative answer

nōs, pron. *we*

nosco, nōvi, nōtum, 3, *ascertain, know*

noster, possess. adj. *our, ours*

nŏta, -ae, f. *mark, brand, infamy*

nŏto, 1, *mark, brand, note*

nōtus, adj. *famous*

nŏverca, -ae, f. *step-mother*

nŏvus, adj. *new, strange*

nox, noctis, f. *night*

noxa, -ae, f. *harm, guilt*

nūbo, nupsi, nuptum, 3, *wed*

nūdus, adj. *naked, bare*

nullus, adj. *no, none*

nūmen, -ĭnis, n. *god, godhead, divine power*

nŭmĕro, 1, *count*

nŭmĕrus, -i, m. *number, metre*

nunc, adv. *now*

nuntius (f. -a), *messenger*

nūper, adv. *lately*

nuptus (f. -a), *bridegroom, bride*

nŭrus, -ūs, f. *daughter-in-law*

nūtrio, 4, *feed, rear*

nūtrix, -īcis, f. *nurse*

nympha(-e), -ae, f. *nymph, maiden*

o, interj. *O!*

ŏb, prep. *on account of*

obruo (ruo), *overwhelm, cover, bury*

obscūrus, adj. *dark, dim, obscure*

obsĕquium, -i, n. *obedience, submission*

observo, 1, *mark, heed, honour*

obsĭdio, -onis, f. *siege*

obstĭpesco, -ui, 3, *grow benumbed, astonished*

obsto (sto), *hinder, obstruct*

obstrĕpo, -ui, -ĭtum, 3, *splash*

occĭdo (cado), *die*

occŭlo, -ui, -tum, 3, *hide*

occumbo, -cŭbui, -cŭbĭtum, 3, *die*

occŭpo, 1, *seize, fall upon, come upon*

ŏcŭlus, -i, m. *eye*

ōdī, defect. vb. *hate*

ōdium, -i, n. *hatred*

Oetaeus, adj. *of Oeta*

ōlim, adv. *of old, sometimes*

omnis, adj. *all, every*

ŏnus, -ĕris, n. *burden, weight*

ŏpācus, adj. *dim, shady*

ŏpĕrio, -ui, -ertum, 4, *shut, cover*

ŏpĕror, dep. 1, *do service, worship*

oppĭdum, -i, n. *town*

oppōno (pono), *set against, oppose, place upon*

ops, ŏpis, f. *wealth, aid, care, power*

optĭmus, adj. *best, excellent*

ŏpus, -ĕris, n. *work, poem, need*

orbis, -is, m. *circle, world*

ordo, -ĭnis, m. *row, order, rank*

ŏrīgo, -ĭnis, f. *origin, source*

ŏrior, ortus, dep. 4, *arise*

orno, 1, *adorn, honour, equip*

ortus, -ūs, n. *rising, source*

ōs, ōris, n. *mouth, face, speech*

ŏs, ossis, n. *bone*

ostreum, -i, n. *oyster*

ŏvis, -is, f. *sheep*

paenĕ, adv. *almost*

paenĭtet, impers. *it repents*

Pălātīnus, adj. *of the Palatine*

pallor, -ōris, m. *paleness*

palma, -ae, f. *palm*

pălūs, -ūdis, f. *marsh*

pānis, -is, m. *bread, loaf*

pār, adj. *like, equal*

părātus (paro), adj. *ready, prepared*

Parcae, -arum, f. *the Fates*

parco, pĕperci, parsum, 3, *spare, forbear*

parcus, adj. *thrifty, scanty*

părens, -tis, c. *parent*

pāreo, -ui, 2, *obey*

pāries, -iĕtis, m. *wall*

părio, pĕpĕri, partum, 3, *bring forth, bear*

păro, 1, *prepare*

pars, -tis, f. *part, rôle*

Parthus, adj. *Parthian*

partim, adv. *partly, in part*

părum, adv. *too little, little*

parvus, adj. *small, slight*

pătella, -ae, f. *small dish*

păteo, -ui, 2, *lie open, am exposed*

păter, -tris, m. *father*

paternus, adj. *paternal*

pătrius, adj. *fatherly, ancestral, native*

pauper, adj. *poor, humble*

păvĭdus, adj. *fearful, timid*

pāvo, -ōnis, m. *peacock*

pax, pācis, f. *peace*

pecto, pexi, pexum, 3, *comb*

pectus, -ŏris, n. *breast, heart, mind*

pĕlăgus, -i, n. *ocean*

pēlex, -ĭcis, f. *mistress*

pello, pĕpŭli, pulsum, 3, *drive, strike*

pĕnātes, -ium, m. *household gods; home*

pendeo, pependi, 2, *hang, am suspended*

pĕr, prep. *through, by means of, on account of*

pĕrăgo (ago), *accomplish, complete*

perdo, -didi, -ditum, 3, *lose, waste*

perdŏceo, -ui, -tum, 2, *teach*

pĕreo (eo), *perish, am wasted, am lost*

perfĭdus, adj. *faithless, treacherous*

perpĕtuus, adj. *perpetual, continuous*

persōna, -ae, f. *mask*

pertĭmesco, -timui, 3, *fear*

pervĕnio (venio), *arrive, reach*

pervĭgĭlo, 1, *watch through*

pervŏlo, 1, *fly, fly through*

pēs, pĕdis, m. *foot*

pĕto, -īvi, -ītum, 3, *seek, make for, attack, woo*

phărĕtra, -ae, f. *quiver*

Phīnēius, adj. *of Phineus*

Phryx, Phrȳgis, adj. *Phrygian*

Pĭĕrĭdes, -um, f. *the Muses*

pĭĕtās, -ātis, f. *affection, duty, love*

pignus, -ŏris, n. *pledge, keepsake, relic*

pĭla, -ae, f. *ball*

pingo, pinxi, pictum, 3, *paint, represent*

pinguis, adj. *fat, fertile*

pinna, -ae, f. *feather, wing*

piscis, -is, m. *fish*

pistor, -ōris, m. *baker*

pĭus, adj. *pious, dutiful, affectionate*

plăceo, -ui, -ĭtum, 2, *please*; impers. *it seems good*

plăcĭdus, adj. *calm, peaceful*

plāco, 1, *appease, calm*

plăga, -ae, f. *net, snare*

plaustrum, -i, n. *wagon*

plebs, plēbis, f. *common people*

plēnus, adj. *full, inspired*

plūs, adv. *more*

plŭvius, adj. *rainy*

poena, -ae, f. *punishment, retribution*

Poenus, adj. *Punic*

pollens, adj. *strong, flourishing*

pŏlus, -i, m. *pole, sky*

pompa, -ae, f. *procession, pomp*

pōno, pŏsui, pŏsĭtum, 3, *place, set up, lay aside, found*

pons, pontis, m. *bridge*

pontĭfex, -ĭcis, m. *pontifex*

pontus, -i, m. *sea*

pŏpŭlus, -i, m. *people*

porca, -ae, f. *sow*

porrĭgo (rego), *stretch out, reach*

porta, -ae, f. *gate*

portĭcus, -ūs, f. *porch, portico*

portus, -ūs, m. *harbour*

possĭdeo, -sēdi, -sessum, 2, *occupy, possess*

post, adv. or prep. *after, behind*

postĕrĭtās, -ātis, f. *posterity*

postĕrus, adj. *coming after, descendant*

postis, -is, m. *post, door-post*

pŏtentia, -ae, f. *sway, influence, power*

pōtus, adj. *drunken, drunk*

praebeo, 2, *afford, supply, offer, render*

praeceptor, -ōris, m. *instructor*

praecĭpio (capio), *instruct, dictate*

praecĭpŭē, adv. *especially*

praecompŏsĭtus, adj. *premeditated*

praeda, -ae, f. *booty, prize*

praefor, -fatum, dep. 1, *address beforehand, preface*

praemium, -i, n. *prize, reward*

praenuntius, adj. *foretelling, heralding*

praepĕs, -pĕtis, c. *bird*

praesens, adj. *present, ready*

praesentia, -ae, f. *presence*

praesignis, adj. *distinguished*

praesto (sto), *excel, maintain, offer*

praeter, prep. *except, besides*

praetereo (eo), *pass by, pass over*

prātum, -i, n. *meadow*

(prex) prĕcis, f. *prayer*

prĕcor, prĕcatus, dep. 1, *pray*

prĕmo, pressi, pressum, 3, *press, be hard upon, check, crush, stamp*

prĕtium, -i, n. *price, value;* in p. esse, *to be esteemed*

prīdem, adv. *formerly, long since*

prīmum, adv. *first, firstly*

prīmus, adj. *first*

princeps, -ĭpis, c. *first, chief*

princĭpium, -i, n. *beginning, source*

priscus, adj. *ancient*

prīvātus, adj. *private, unofficial*

prō, prep. *in front of, instead of, in return for*

prŏbo, 1, *test, prove, approve, make good*

prŏbus, adj. *honest, upright*

prōcumbo (cumbo), *fall before, grovel, bow*

prōcurro (curro), *jut out, project, run forward*

prŏcus, -i, m. *suitor*

prŏfānus, adj. *secular, profane*

prōfĭteor, -fessus, dep. 2, *profess, confess*

profundo, -fudi, -fūsum, 3, *pour out, lavish*

prōlēs, -is, f. *offspring, race, descendants*

prōmo, prompsi, promptum, 3, *produce, draw forth*

prŏpĕ, adv. and prep. *near, nearly*

prŏpĕro, 1, *hasten, make quickly*

prŏpinquus, adj. *neighbouring, related*

propter, prep. *near, on account of*

prōsĕco, -ui, -tum, 1, *cut off*

prōsĭlio, -ui, 4, *leap forth*

prosper, -a, -um, adj. *prosperous, favourable*

prospĭcio, -spexi, -spectum, 3, *look forth, look at*

prōsum (sum), *benefit, do good*

prōtĭnus, adv. *forthwith*

prōvŏco, 1, *call forth, challenge*
prōvŏlo, 1, *fly forth*
proxĭmus, adj. *next, nearest*
prŭīna, -ae, f. *hoar-frost*
pŭblĭcus, adj. *public, official*
pŭdet, impers. vb. *it shames*
pŭdor, -ōris, m. *shame, modesty, honour*
pŭer, -i, m. *boy*
pŭĕrīlis, adj. *boyish, youthful*
pugna, -ae, f. *battle, encounter*
pugno, 1, *fight, strive*
pulcher, -chra, -chrum, adj. *beautiful, splendid*
pulso, 1, *beat, strike*
pūmĭceus, adj. *of pumice-stone*
puppis, -is, f. *poop*
purgāmen, -ĭnis, n. *washing, off-scouring*
purgo, 1, *purify*
purpŭrĕus, adj. *purple*
pūrus, adj. *pure, plain*
pŭto, 1, *think*
Pygmaeus, adj. *of the Pygmies*

quā, adv. *where, by what road, in so far as*
quaero, quaesīvi, quaestum (quaesitum), 3, *ask, seek, look for*
quālis, pron. adj. *of what kind*
quam, adv. *than, how*
quamvīs, adj. and conj. *as much as you will, though*
quantum, adv. *as much, so much*
quantus, adj. *how great, as great*
quantuslĭbet, adj. *as great as you will*
quārē, adv. *how*
quartus, adj. *fourth*
quătĕr, num. adv. *four times*
quătio, no perf., quassum, 3, *shake, strike, break*
-quĕ, conj. *and*
quĕror, questus, dep. 3, *complain, lament*
quī, rel. pron. *who, which*
quī (quĭs), interr. pron. *who? which? what?*
quĭa, conj. *because*
quĭcunque, pron. *whosoever*

quīdam, pron. *a certain, some one*
quĭdem, adv. *indeed, at any rate*
quĭēs, -ētis, f. *rest, peace*
quinque, indecl. adj. *five*
quintus, adj. *fifth*
Quĭrīnālis, adj. *of Quirinus, Quirinal*
Quĭrītes, -ium, m. *Quirites, Roman citizens*
quisque, pron. *each*
quisquis, pron. *whosoever*
quīvis, pron. *any you please*
quō, adv. and conj. *whither, to what end?*
quod, conj. *because*
quondam, adv. *formerly, once*
quŏquĕ, conj. *also, too, even*
quot, indecl. adj. *how many, as many*

răcēmĭfer, -a, -um, adj. *grape-bearing*
rădius, -i, m. *ray, spoke*
răpīna, -ae, f. *pillage, robbery, booty*
răpio, rapui, raptum, 3, *seize, carry off, rob, snatch*
rārus, adj. *infrequent*
rĕbello, 1, *rebel, renew war*
rĕcēdo (cedo), *retire, retreat, pass out*
rĕcens, adj. *fresh, recent*
rĕcessus, -ūs, m. *retreat, retirement*
rĕcĭpio (capio), *retire, take back, receive, take in, affirm*
rĕcurvus, adj. *curved*
reddo, -didi, -ditum, 3, *render, give back, pay*
rĕdeo (eo), *return*
rĕdĭmio, 4, *wreathe, deck*
rĕdundo, 1, *overflow, fall back upon*
rĕdux, adj. *returning, restored*
rĕfĕro (fero), *bring back, relate, refer, reflect*
rĕfulgeo, -fulsi, -fulsum, 2, *shine, glitter*
rēgālis, adj. *regal, royal*
rēgia, -ae, f. *palace*
rēgīna, -ae, f. *queen*
rēgio, -onis, f. *region, place*
rēgius, adj. *kingly*

regnum, -i, n. *realm, kingly power*

rĕlinquo, -līqui, -lictum, 3, *leave, abandon*

rĕmitto (mitto), *admit, drop, let go, send back*

rĕmŏror, -atus, dep. 1, *hang back, detain*

rĕmōtus, adj. *distant*

rĕmŏveo, -mōvi, -mōtum, 2, *remove, withdraw*

rĕneo, 2, *unspin, reverse*

rĕor, rătus, dep. 2, *think*

rĕpello (pello), *drive back, repel*

rĕpĕrio, reppĕri, -pertum, 3, *find, discover*

rĕquiro (quaero), *seek, look in vain for, ask*

rēs, rei, f. *thing, object, affair, work, theme,* &c.

rĕsīdo, -sēdi, 3, *sit down, settle, sink*

rĕsigno, 1, *unseal, reveal, resign*

rĕsisto, -stĭti, -stĭtum, 3, *resist, halt, stand still*

rĕsolvo, -vi, -utum, 3, *open*

respicio, -spexi, -spectum, 3, *regard, consider, look back*

respondeo, -spondi, -sponsum, 2, *answer, correspond to*

resto, -stiti, 1, *remain over, abide*

rĕtĭneo (teneo), *hold back, keep, check*

rĕvello, -velli, -vulsum, 3, *pluck out, tear away*

rĕvēlo, 1, *unveil, disclose*

rĕvertor, -versus, dep. 3, *return*

rĕvinco (vinco), *conquer, refute*

rex, rēgis, m. *king*

rĭgĭdus, adj. *stiff, hard*

rīpa, -ae, f. *bank*

rītus, -ūs, m. *rite*

rŏgo, 1, *ask*

rŏgus, -i, m. *bier, grave*

Rōmānus, adj. *Roman*

rōs, rōris, m. *dew*

rostrum, -i, n. *beak,* pl. *Rostra*

rŏta, -ae, f. *wheel*

rŏtundus, adj. *round*

rŭber, -bra, -brum, adj. *red*

rubesco, rubui, 3, *blush, grow red*

rŭbĭcundus, adj. *ruddy*

rŭdo, -īvi, -ītum, 3, *bray*

rūmor, -ōris, m. *rumour, fame*

rŭo, rŭi, rŭtum, 3, *rush, fall down, dash down*

rūs, rūris, n. *country*

rustĭcus, adj. *of the country*

Săbīnus, adj. *Sabine*

săcer, -cra, -crum, adj. *sacred, inspired*

săcerdos, -dōtis, m. *priest*

săcrĭfĭco, 1, *sacrifice*

săcrĭfĭcus, adj. *sacrificial*

săcro, 1, *consecrate*

săcrum, -i, n. *rite, worship, sacred object*

saepĕ, adv. *often*

saevus, adj. *cruel, fierce*

sălix, -ĭcis, f. *willow*

sălūber, -bris, -bre, adj. *wholesome, beneficial*

sălūs, -ūtis, f. *safety, salvation, welfare*

sanctus, adj. *sacred*

sanguĭnŏlentus, adj. *bloody, bloodstained*

sanguis, -ĭnis, m. *blood, bloodshed*

sătĭs, adv. *enough, fairly*

Sāturnius, adj. *of Saturn*

sătyrus, -i, m. *satyr*

saxum, -i, n. *rock, stone*

scăber, -bra, -brum, adj. *rough*

scaena, -ae, f. *stage, scene*

scamnus, -i, m. *bench*

scĕlĕrātus, adj. *wicked*

scĕlus, -ĕris, n. *crime*

sceptrĭfer, -a, -um, adj. *sceptre-bearing*

sceptrum, -i, n. *sceptre*

scīlĭcet, adv. *surely, to be sure, forsooth*

scio, 4, *know*

scirpea, -ae, f. *rush-basket*

scŏpŭlus, -i, m. *crag, cliff*

scūtum, -i, n. *shield*

sē, pron. *one's self*

sēcēdo (cedo), m. *am distant*

sēcerno, -crēvi, -crētum, 3, *separate, distinguish*

sĕco, -ui, -tum, 1, *cut, slay*

sēcrētus (secerno), adj. *secret, set apart*

sĕcundus, adj. *second, favourable*

sēcūrus, adj. *secure, care-free*

sĕd, conj. *but*

sĕdeo, sēdi, sessum, 3, *sit*

sēdes, -is, f. *seat, abode*

sēdo, 1, *allay, settle*

sēdŭlĭtas, -ātis, f. *zeal, officiousness*

sēdŭlus, adj. *busy, zealous*

sĕgĕs, -ĕtis, f. *corn-field, crops*

sĕmel, adv. *once*

sēmen, -ĭnis, n. *seed*

semper, adv. *always*

sĕnecta, -ae, f.,

sĕnectūs, -ūtis, f. *old age*

sĕnesco, sĕnui, 3, *grow old*

sĕnex, sĕnis, m. *old man*

sentio, sensi, sensum, 4, *feel, perceive*

septem, indecl. adj. *seven*

septĭmus, adj. *seventh*

sĕquor, secūtus, dep. 3, *follow, scour*

sĕrēnus, adj. *calm, clear*

sĕrō, sēvi, sătum, 3, *sow*

sērō, adv. *late*

sertum, -i, n. *garland*

servio, 4, *serve*

servo, 1, *save, preserve*

servus (f. -a), m. *slave*

seu, conj. *or if, whether*

sex, indecl. adj. *six*

sextus, adj. *sixth*

sī, conj. *if*

sīc, adv. *so, thus*

siccus, adj. *dry*

sīcut, adv. *as if, just as*

signĭfĭco, 1, *represent, symbolise, intimate*

signum, -i, n. *sign, proof, standard*

sĭmĭlis, adj. *like*

sĭmul, adv. and conj. *at the same time, as soon as*

sĭmŭlācrum, -i, n. *likeness, portrait*

sĭnĕ, prep. *without*

sĭno, sīvi, sĭtum, 3, *allow, leave*

sisto, stĭti, stĭtum, 3, *make to stand, set up, stop*

sīvĕ, see seu

sōbrius, adj. *sober*

sŏcer, -cri, m. *father-in-law*

sŏcius, adj. *allied with, associated with*

sōl, -is, m. *sun*

sŏleo, solĭtus, semi-dep. 2, *am accustomed*

sŏlĭdus, adj. *whole, unbroken*

sŏlium, -i, n. *throne*

sollemnis, adj. *solemn, customary*

sollĭcĭto, 1, *worry, tease, importune*

sollĭcĭtus, adj. *anxious, careful*

solstĭtiālis, adj. *of the solstice, midsummer*

sŏlum, -i, n. *ground, floor*

sōlus, adj. *alone, lonely*

solvo, solvi, solūtum, 3, *loose, release, give up, pay*

somnus, -i, m. *sleep*

sŏno, -ui, -ĭtum, 1, *sound, clatter*

sŏnus, -i, m. *sound, word*

sŏror, -ōris, f. *sister*

sors, sortis, f. *lot, destiny, child*

sospēs, adj. *safe*

spargo, sparsi, sparsum, 3, *sprinkle, scatter*

spătium, -i, n. *space, room, scope, period*

spĕcĭēs, -ēi, f. *appearance, guise, beauty*

spēs, spēi, f. *hope, promise*

spīna, -ae, f. *thorn*

stagnum, -i, n. *pond*

stătua, -ae, f. *statue*

stătuo, -ui, -ūtum, 3, *set up, determine*

stella, -ae, f. *star*

sterno, strāvi, strātum, 3, *lay low, spread, besprinkle*

stĭmŭlus, -i, m. *goad, point*

stĭpŭla, -ae, f. *straw, thatch*

stirps, stirpis, f. *stock, stem, race*

sto, stĕti, stătum, 1, *stand, stare, be fixed*

stŏla, -ae, f. *gown*

strīdeo (strido), 2 or 3, *screech*

strix, strĭgis, f. *screech-owl*

stŭdium, -i, n. *zeal, effort, attachment*

stultus, adj. *foolish*

suādeo, suāsi, suāsum, 2, *persuade*

sŭb, prep. *under, beneath*

sŭbeo (eo), *go under, approach, occur*

sŭbĭcio (iacio), *place beneath, subject to*

sŭbĭtō, adv. *suddenly*

sŭbĭtus, adj. *sudden*

subsēco (seco), *cut away*

subsum (sum), *am under, am at hand*

sŭburbānus, adj. *of a neighbouring town, neighbouring*

subverto, -i, -sum, 3, *overturn, ruin*

succumbo (cumbo), *be subject to, lie down under*

succurro (curro), *bring help to, run to, occur*

summus, adj. *topmost, top of;* **summa** (n. pl.), *top, crown*

sūmo, sumpsi, sumptum, 3, *take, don, assume*

sŭper, adv. and prep. *over, above*

sŭperbus, adj. *proud*

sŭperi, -um, m. *gods* (of the upper world)

sŭperiniectus, adj. *placed above*

sŭpero, I, *surpass*

supersum (sum), *survive, am left over*

suppōno (pono), *put under, make subject to*

sŭprēmus, adj. *highest, topmost*

surgo, surrexi, surrectum, 3, *arise*

sūs, suis, c. *pig*

suscĭpio (capio), *take up, undertake*

suspensus, adj. *suspended, wavering*

sustĭneo (teneo), *endure, hold up, hold out*

suus, possess. adj. *his, her, its*

Sўrācōsius, adj. *Syracusan*

tăcĭtus, adj. *silent*

taeda, -ae. f. *torch, marriage*

tālis, adj. *such, of such a kind*

tam, adv. *so*

tămĕn, conj. *but, yet*

tantum, adv. *so much, merely*

tantummŏdŏ, adv. *merely, only*

tantus, adj. *so great, of such a size*

Taurīnus, adj. *of the Bull*

taurus, -i, m. *bull*

tectum, -i, n. *roof, building*

Tēgĕaeus, adj. *of Tegea*

tĕgo, texi, tectum, 3, *cover, conceal*

tĕgŭla, -ae, f. *tile*

tellūs, -ūris, f. *earth*

tēlum, -i, n. *weapon, javelin*

tĕmĕrārius, adj. *rash, heedless*

tĕmĕrē, adv. *rashly, at random*

tĕmĕro, I, *defile*

tempestas, -ātis, f. *weather, storm*

templum, -i, n. *temple*

tempus, -ŏris, n. *time, season, forehead*

tendo, tĕtendi, tensum, 3, *stretch, aim, strive*

tĕneo, -ui, -tum, 2, *hold, keep, restrain, understand*

tĕpĭdus, adj. *warm*

tĕr, adv. *thrice*

tĕrĕbro, I, *bore*

tergum, -i, n. *back*

ternus, distributive num. *three each, three*

tĕro, trīvi, trītum, 3, *wear, waste, rub, grind*

terra, -ae, f. *earth*

terreo, 2, *frighten*

tertius, adj. *third*

testis, -is, c. *witness*

texo, texui, textum, 3, *weave, twine*

thălămus, -i, m. *chamber, couch, marriage*

Thēbānus, adj. *Theban*

thŏlus, -i, m. *dome*

tībia, -ae, f. *pipe, flute*

tībĭcĕn, -ĭnis, m. } *flute-player*
tībĭcĭna, -ae, f. }

tĭmeo, 2, *fear*

tĭmĭdē, adv. *timidly*

tĭmĭdus, adj. *timid, fearful*

tĭmor, -ōris, m. *fear*

tinguo, tinxi, tinctum, 3, *dip, dye*

tĭtŭbo, 1, *stagger, stammer*

tĭtŭlus, -i, m. *title, inscription, cause*

tŏga, -ae, f. *toga*

tollo, sustŭli, sublātum, 3, *uplift, remove, do away*

Tŏnans, *Thunderer* (epithet of Jupiter)

torreo, -ui, tostum, 2, *roast, parch*

tŏrus, -i, m. *couch, marriage, bier*

tostus (torreo), adj. *roast, cooked*

tŏt, indecl. adj. *so many*

tŏtĭdem, indecl. adj. *just so many*

tōtus, adj. *whole, entire, wrapped up in*

trăbĕa, -ae, f. *striped robe*

trādo, -didi, -ditum, 3, *report, yield*

trăho, traxi, tractum, 3, *lead astray, draw, derive*

transfero (fero), *carry over, transfer*

Trăsĭmēnus, adj. *of Trasimene*

trĕmo, -ui, 3, *tremble, fear*

trēs, indecl. num. *three*

tristis, adj. *sad, gloomy, unfavourable*

trĭumphālis, adj. *triumphal*

trĭumphus, -i, m. *triumph*

trux, trŭcis, adj. *fierce*

tū, pron. *thou*

tŭeor, dep. 2, *guard, watch*

tŭmŭlo, 1, *bury*

turba, -ae, f. *crowd, confusion*

turpis, adj. *base, ugly*

turrĭger, adj. *tower-crowned*

turris, -is, f. *tower*

tūs, tūris, n. *incense*

Tuscus, adj. *Tuscan*

tūtus, adj. *safe*

tuus, possess. pron. *thy, thine*

tympănum, -i, n. *timbrel*

ŭbĭ, conj. *where, when*

ūdus, adj. *wet*

ultĭmus, adj. *last, farthest*

ultor, -ōris, m. *avenger*

ŭlŭlātus, -ūs, m. *shrieking*

umbra, -ae, f. *shade*

ūmĭdus, adj. *moist*

unda, -ae, f. *wave*

undĕ, conj. *whence, by what means*

unguis, -is, m. *claw, hoof, nail*

ūnĭcus, adj. *sole, unique*

ūnus, adj. *one*

urbs, urbis, f. *city*

urgeo, ursi, 3, *push, drive, oppress*

ursa, -ae, f. *she-bear*

ūsus, -ūs, m. *use, experience, habit*

ŭt(-ī), conj. *in order that, so that, as, when, how*

ūterque, pron. *each of two, both*

ūtĭlis, adj. *useful, serviceable*

ŭtĭnam, adv. *would that!*

ūtor, ūsus, dep. 3, *use, employ*

uxor, -is, f. *wife*

vacca, -ae, f. *cow*

Văcūnālis, adj. *of Vacuna*

văcuus, adj. *empty, idle, vain, free*

vādo, 3, *go*

vāgio, 4, *whimper*

văgus, adj. *wandering, indefinite, at large*

văleo, 2, *am strong*; imper. and subj. *farewell!*

vălĭdus, adj. *strong, heady*

vallis, -is, f. *valley*

vātes, -is, m. *bard, prophet*

-vĕ, conj. *or*

vĕho, vexi, vectum, 3, *carry, convey, sail*

vel, conj. *or*

vēlāmen, -ĭnis, n. *covering, garment*

vēlo, 1, *veil, cover*

vēlox, adj. *swift*

vĕnio, vēni, ventum, 4, *come*

verbum, -i, n. *word*

vĕreor, vĕrĭtus, dep. 2, *fear*

verso, 1, *turn*

vertex, -ĭcis, m. *crown, eddy*

vērus, adj. *true, right*

Vestālis, adj. *of Vesta, Vestal*

vester, possess. adj. *yours*

vestĭbŭlum, -i, n. *fore-court*

vestis, -is, f. *garment*

vĕto, -ui, -ĭtum, 1, *forbid*

vĕtŭs, -ĕris, adj. *old*

vĕtustus, adj. *old*

vexo, 1, *harass, ravage*

vĭa, -ae, f. *way, road, journey*

vĭcīnus, adj. *neighbouring*
victĭma, -ae, f. *victim*
victor, -ōris, m. *conqueror*
victus, -ūs, m. *livelihood, food*
vīcus, -i, m. *street, quarter, village*
vĭdeo, vīdi, vīsum, 2, *see, understand, provide*
vĭgĭl, adj. *watchful, sleepless*
vĭgor, -ōris, m. *vigour*
vīmen, -ĭnis, n. *osier*
vindex, -ĭcis, m. *champion*
vindĭco, 1, *protect, avenge, claim*
vindicta, -ae, f. *act of freeing*
vīnum, -i, n. *wine*
vĭŏla, -ae, f. *violet*
vĭŏlo, 1, *violate, disfigure*
vĭr, -i, m. *man, bridegroom, husband*
virga, -ae, f. *rod*
virgĭnĕus, adj. *maidenly*
virgĭnĭtas, -ātis, f. *virginity*
virgo, -ĭnis, f. *virgin, maiden*
vĭrĭdis, adj. *green*
virtūs, -ūtis, f. *virtue, courage*

vīs, f. *force, strength*
viscŭs, -ĕris, n. *entrails, flesh*
vīta, -ae, f. *life*
vĭtio, 1, *stain, defile*
vitta, -ae, f. *head-band, fillet*
vīvo, vixi, victum, 3, *live*
vīvus, adj. *alive, fresh*
vix, adv. *scarcely*
vŏco, 1, *call, invite, challenge*
volgus, -i, n. *crowd, common folk*
volnus, -ĕris, n. *wound, harm*
vŏlo, 1, *fly*
vŏlo, -ui, 3, *wish, mean*
Volscus, adj. *Volscian*
voltus, -ūs, m. *face, countenance*
vŏlūbĭlĭtas, -tātis, f. *roundness*
vŏlŭcer, -cris, -cre, adj. *winged*
volŭcris, -is, f. *bird*
vōs, pron. *you*
vōtum, -i, n. *prayer, vow*
vox, vōcis, f. *voice, utterance*

Zĕphўrus, -i, m. *west wind*
Zōna, -ae, f. *belt of Orion*

GENERAL AND GRAMMATICAL INDEX, &c.

INDEX OF NAMES: TOPOGRAPHY, HISTORY, &c.

CAMBRIDGE: PRINTED BY W. LEWIS, M.A., AT THE UNIVERSITY PRESS